Putting GOD to WORK

Putting GOD to WORK

Living God's Principles @ Work

Scott Neil MacLellan

Dawson**Media**

ISBN: 978-1-61291-150-2

Cover design by WhiteHouse Advertising & Design

Some of the anecdotal illustrations in this book are true to life and are included with the permission of the persons involved. All other illustrations are composites of real situations, and any resemblance to people living or dead is coincidental.

Unless otherwise identified, all Scripture quotations in this publication are taken from THE HOLY BIBLE, NEW INTERNATIONAL VERSION®, (NIV®). Copyright © 1973, 1978, 1984 by Biblica, Inc.™ Used by permission. All rights reserved worldwide. The other version used is the King James Version (KJV).

MacLellan, Scott Neil.
  Putting God to work : living God's principles @ work / Scott Neil MacLellan.
    p. cm.
  ISBN 978-1-61291-150-2
  1. Employees—Religious life. 2. Work—Religious aspects—Christianity. I. Title.
  BV4593.M23 2011
  248.8'8—dc23
                                    2011041364

Printed in the United States of America

1 2 3 4 5 6 7 8 / 15 14 13 12 11

Contents

A Note About the Title

The title of this book is intended to be provocative. To take the title literally, however, puts God in a subservient position, which is obviously the opposite of the message I'm looking to convey.

Over the years, I have heard so many people say, "I've prayed for this or that, but God is not answering my prayers." This book is intended to explain why those prayers might have gone unanswered. It is intended to show how God has answered prayers as articulated in the Bible. It is also intended to outline how Christ lived his own life as shown to us in the Bible. If we can model these principles, most of which are based on glorifying God and serving others, then God will give to us so that we can give to others. This, in effect, puts the power of God to work in our lives, including in the workplace.

In reality, we need not do anything other than accept Christ to receive forgiveness for our sins. Grace means that we cannot earn forgiveness, so there is nothing in this book that you need to follow to get into heaven. God will not love us any more if we do these things or any less if we don't do these things. These ten principles simply guide us to grow in our faith and to allow Christ to live through us in the workplace. As we learn to submit and allow more of Christ to flow through us at work, God moves in and takes over. Because Christ has been anointed, we become anointed. Good things cannot help but follow. In effect, we "put God to work" because it is truly God who shows up to work every day, not you. Pretty cool!

The Basement Breakthrough

What makes you think I am somehow separate from your work?
These are the words I heard so clearly while praying about my job situation one evening. They would begin a journey that would lead me to experience God's forgiveness and to apply his abundance to the very work environment I was looking to escape.

I'll tell you more about that later. First, let me give you a little background on what led me to that conversation with God in the first place.

Eighteen months earlier, my friends and I had sold our two-year-old start-up company to a multinational corporation. The negotiations were tough, and by the time of the sale we were all ready for a change of scenery. We had worked most of the previous two years (including most weekends) without a break, and by now we just wanted to "chill-ax," as my daughters would say. I was ready to go play for a while.

As CEO of our company, however, I felt that it was my responsibility to stay on with the new firm for a short time in order to properly transition the business and ensure that the people who had helped grow us into a sellable enterprise were smoothly integrated into the acquiring company's culture. It would have been unfair to our great team if we just sold them off and hit the beach. It also would have been unprofessional for me to cut and run from the acquiring company without helping them get value from the business they had just purchased. So I put on my big-boy pants, pulled myself together, and went back to work to get the business settled.

I was very happy with the new company. They were great people and great business partners, and our company thrived with their additional support. It was a perfect fit. But now, a year and a half later, I'd done all I thought I could do. It seemed time to move on to a new undertaking. Something else was pulling at me.

Basement Breakthrough

Someone had given me the book *Halftime* by Bob Buford, and while reading it I had convinced myself (perhaps incorrectly) that it was time to step off the corporate treadmill and focus exclusively on serving God. I wanted to do something kingdom-minded. I had been praying about moving into my "second half" yet had received no clear guidance about any particular new path.

I must not get it, I began to think. *Clearly I'm just not committed enough to my faith.* I was very frustrated and confused about what to do. This went on for many months.

Then one evening I was in my basement exercising when I suddenly felt compelled to pray. So I hopped off the stationary bicycle and got down on my knees. Not quite sure what to pray about, I started with my usual custom of praying for family. Then my prayers turned to my work. Admittedly, over the course of the past year my supplications to God had pretty much turned to complaints about why I was working when I could be doing something more to serve Him.

I had gotten really, really good at the complaining part. I could just imagine the lunchroom chatter in heaven about me: "Look out! Scott's starting to pray again!" They probably drew straws each time to determine who would have to listen to me. But on this particular evening I think the Holy Spirit stepped in and said, "I've got this one."

So there I was, complaining to God again, when something hit me. Hard. Something came over me that made me perfectly still. It's hard to describe, but it was almost as though something sucked all the thoughts out of my head and held me in place. I felt almost paralyzed and stayed that way for a minute or two.

Imagine total silence, total quiet in your mind, no feeling in your body, no movement of any kind — and I mean *any kind*. That's when it happened. It was so clear that I almost heard the words out loud, although it was more like a thought that was so lucid it was unmistakable as a message:

What makes you think I am somehow separate from your work?

What was that? Who was that? What does it mean? Did I just get a revelation from God, or do I belong on *Jerry Springer*?

Stunned, I stayed there on my knees for what felt like half an hour. I'm not sure if I thought anything else, felt anything else, or said anything else. Gradually, I seemed to come to and return to my normal state. I turned around and sat on the floor for the next hour, trying to process what had just happened. I felt as though I'd been hit upside the head by an angel with a two-by-four.

In retrospect, I think that's exactly what happened. God had been sending me subtle messages all along, but it took this kind of dramatic intervention for me to actually hear what he was saying. It took an Acme anvil to the face for me to actually stop and pay attention. And pay attention I did. It was impossible not to. God had just spoken to me — how do you ignore that?

All this time I had been itching to serve God in a new situation . . . when God wanted me to serve him right where I was.

I had convinced myself that God was not part of my working life, that he and I had a sort of mutual agreement that my business should be compartmentalized from my faith. But now, suddenly, I saw that God is part of every aspect of my life. It was only my limited view of how God works that had caused me to think that he was not part of wherever I happened to be at the moment or that I had to leave my present environment in order to more effectively serve him.

His desire, his plan, was to work through me right where I was.

God Is . . . Wherever You Are

Shortly after that night, I found myself on a path that would make me CEO of a $2.2 billion division of the company that had acquired our business. Things have gone very well since then. I work with great people, and I love what I do. Our team has been overwhelmingly successful, and at one point our results were among the best in the world.

But my personal career is not the focus of this book. I will tell stories on myself—mostly to illustrate what *not* to do in your own career. I'll also share with you some of my journey of self-discovery. Your personal path will bring its own unique discoveries, but my hope is that I can share a helpful signpost or two to help you make the most of your journey.

The objective of *Putting God to Work* is to show you how to apply ten principles I've learned to your own life at work as well as at home. The message of the book is that *God is part of every life situation, including our work*. The only question is our willingness to recognize him as part of our daily circumstances. God's goodness and mercy are there for all to access at any time and in any place. We don't have to be on a mission trip in a distant country to be serving God. We can serve God wherever we are.

I still think that going on a mission trip is an awesome and loving thing to do, but we can be on a mission trip wherever we are at any given time. You are on a mission trip when you listen to a coworker who's hurting. You are on a mission trip as the only Christian in a very secular company. You are on a mission trip with your atheist spouse. And you are on a mission trip with your rebellious children.

On a related note, although this book will focus on your work situation, the things we will talk about also apply to every aspect of your life. The same ideas that are effective on the job are equally effective with your spouse, your children, your parents, and your friends. If you are looking for joy and abundance at work, I'll assume that you'd like joy and abundance in your home life as well. Because God does not distinguish between work and home life—he's everywhere and has the same expectations in every situation—the rules work wherever you are.

To be honest, I'm still absorbing that message into my own life.

It took me virtually all of the next ten years since that fateful night in my basement to see some of what God was trying to show me about his presence at work and with my family. I'm sure that if you asked my wife, children, and coworkers about me, they would emphatically state that I'm still a big (as in HUGE) work in progress.

I mess up all the time—and I really mean *all the time*! I still think that I'm the one producing results. I continue to look to my own self-determination to get the job done, often forgetting that God is the most powerful resource I could ever bring into my workplace and family. It's like having a winning lottery ticket in my pocket but living in poverty. The resources are right there. I only have to remember to use them.

God has gradually put me in the right places with the right people to help me see how I can best serve him and to help me understand what he wants to accomplish through me. He has gradually shown me that when I seek first his kingdom and his righteousness, abundance follows. Results are not generated from self. *Results are generated from looking past self.* God is not Santa Claus or a genie in a bottle. But he does watch over, protect, and bless those who honor and obey him.

Journey of a Lifetime

I am on a journey of discovery that will last a lifetime. I am only just beginning to realize his grace at work and at home. I am only beginning to see how to serve God among the people I work with every day. I'm still not very good at it, but at the very least I'm starting to see how much I miss the mark. Before, I was just oblivious to it.

The ten principles I want to share with you have been learned mostly the hard way, from doing things wrong rather than right. The good results I've managed to pull together in my career are mostly through grace or by learning from other people who have been wonderful mentors and bosses to me. Even today, knowing what I have now come to understand, I continually mess up despite my best intentions. I have, in many ways, succeeded in spite of myself.

In the end, that might be the most important message of all. *Most of what God does through us, he does only after we realize our inadequacies and get out of his way.* It is usually only after we are brought to our knees and turn our circumstances over to God that the right solution makes itself known. Surrender is the clearest path to victory. When we use our own intelligence, we can obtain one level of success. But when we empty ourselves and defer to the heart of God, our potential is limitless.

I confess that, as a business executive, deferring to God's heart was a tough lesson for me to learn. People like me think that we rise to the top of the corporate ladder through our own hard work, ambition, determination, and intelligence. As the world sees it, this might be true. But that kind of success is temporary and fickle. It is not our ambition or our cleverness that wins in the long run. It is something much larger than that. Sustainable success happens only when we deny ourselves and let God do the work.

It is in that "something much larger" that I now place my trust. *Trust* is a strong word. It implies faith, certainty, assurance, and conviction. It is so much more than mere belief, for belief comes and goes as circumstances change. Trust and assurance, on the other hand, are constant and unchangeable. So my hope is that this book will not only inspire you but that it will also awaken and deepen your trust in the God who loves you so much that he wants only goodness and mercy from you and for you in every aspect of your life.

God bless.

Acknowledgments

What greater thanks could I give than the thanks that go to Christ, who paid the ultimate price for me so that my sins would be crucified on the cross and I would be made blameless before God?

To the Holy Spirit. I am so grateful that you have worked in my life to give me revelation. Your presence has been so powerful that I cannot even express it in words.

And to my God, who has paved the way before me. My Creator and my all in all. We are here to glorify you. Thank you for giving me a small glimpse into you and for creating a hunger in me to seek you without ceasing.

To my family, starting with my mother and father for loving me so much and teaching me so many important values. To my sister, who showed me what selfless love is while I was growing up. To my wife, who is my joy and the love of my life. To my daughters, who have taught me more about life than I could have ever learned in many life-times without them. I am forever grateful for your presence in my life, and I love you, love you, love you.

To Dave, who was there when I was baptized by the Spirit and who invested in me without any expectation of anything in return.

To Mark, who pursued me in Christ long before I was ready to listen and who made important contributions to this book.

To my good friend George, who has shown me what it is like to really love everyone with whom you come in contact.

To Ryan, who inspired me to pursue this ministry.

To Monica and the entire team at White House Advertising & Design. They dedicated countless hours to this book, making it look better and more professional than I could have possibly hoped for.

And to Dan, who has been an important guide in editing the book while offering critical counsel in taking this book to market.

None of us gets anywhere without the blessing of God and the support of many good friends and mentors. My life has been filled with many teachers, many supporters, many great bosses, and thousands of awesome team members from whom I learn every day. You are the reason I get excited about coming to work.

This book is dedicated to all of you.

Patience for the Journey

There is a military axiom that basically says no battle plan survives first contact with the enemy. Likewise, in the working world I've found that no business plan survives first contact with coworkers, customers, or competitors. Even when you seek to put God first in your working life, your plan, no matter how noble, is likely to escape you the moment you make first contact with work on Monday morning.

Regardless of how determined you are to bring God with you to your workplace, it's very possible that you will default to your human nature as soon as the world makes contact with you. And this is true even in friendly situations. Your human nature is, after all, what you know best. You have relied on your own hard work and intelligence your entire life. It will take you time and practice to start relying on something else—or, rather, someone else.

Just as Peter denied Jesus three times in the face of a hostile mob, chances are, especially at first, that you're going to forget your higher purpose as soon as your boss asks you a question or a coworker comments on your current project or a customer says your account is at risk. When presented with any work problem, most of us tend to default to our old self and attempt to take on the world as we always have.

But I want to share with you something more powerful than the world and more powerful than human intelligence. I'm talking about tapping into the unmatched power of the Creator of heaven and earth.

Don't judge yourself when you fall short. I've been applying these principles for years and still, even in the mildest of business situations, I often forget who I am and to whom I belong. My mind starts to race, and I immediately default to all the worldly responses that have proven "successful" for me over the years.

It is only through prayer, practice, and patience that I have learned to pause a nanosecond before speaking to ask God for his calm guidance and to reflect his love and intentions through me. In doing so, I'm denying myself, including my human nature and my human mind. That's not easy for someone who for fifty years has believed that it's been *me* making it all happen!

One Principle at a Time

As you journey through this book, I encourage you to take time to reflect on the chapters individually. They are prepared to offer relatively easy-to-digest concepts that you can pray about and put into practice one transformational principle at a time. Each chapter can also serve as a personal Bible study of sorts and even as the basis of a hearty small-group discussion. Each principle blends biblical truth with real-life work situations. It's one thing to study the Word of God; it's another to practice it and put it to work when confronted with the real world. *Putting God to Work* will get you thinking about how God's Word applies to life as we know it today.

Don't rush through this book. Take time to reflect on what you read. You might even determine to meditate on each concept for a week or more before moving on to the next principle. Better yet, get into a study group and talk through each of the ten principles. I'll pose a few questions at the end of each chapter for you to think about, discuss, and pray about. Observe your life honestly in relation to each chapter's precepts to see if your actual behavior matches your desired behavior. Talk through your ideas as well as your struggles with your study group. Synergize insights, learn from each other's experiences, and encourage one another to think, speak, and act as an ambassador of God wherever he has placed you because, indeed, you are his ambassador.

For Leaders in All Walks of Life

Putting God to Work is for people in all walks of life and in all positions of authority. While I will often refer to leadership, my message is not intended only for aspiring CEOs. Some of the best leaders I know don't hold official positions or power. They might or might not have money and might or might not have someone reporting to them. Yet they are leaders of people. I'm speaking of the mom or dad who leads a family, the teacher who leads a classroom, the nurse who leads a patient back to health, the frontline worker who leads her coworkers to greater productivity, the pastor or small-group facilitator who leads people to Christ, the supervisor who leads a small team to completion of multiple projects, and of course the CEO who leads a company through good times and bad times.

If you lead people in any way, large or small, this book is for you.

Together, we're going to explore ten principles that work no matter what challenges you apply them to. You can bring the power, wisdom, creativity, and compassion of God into your workplace and all other aspects of your life if you take the time to trust that he wants all of these things for you.

I invite your comments, your thoughts, and your stories about how you have put God to work. Please visit us at *puttinggodtowork.com*. May God bless your every thought and action in your everyday ministry.

The Sand Hill Shuffle

PRINCIPLE 1: *Grow where you are planted.*

Nevertheless, each one should retain the place in life that the Lord assigned to him and to which God has called him.

— 1 CORINTHIANS 7:17

When a good friend and I first began talking about starting our own company, I already had it pretty good as most people would view it. I was the president of a fairly large organization, making a great salary with solid benefits and a long-term incentive plan that would be worth millions if I could hang on for just another three years.

But something still drove me toward this conversation about branching out on our own. We talked off and on for about six months until we decided to act on the idea. We got up very early one morning and flew out to San Francisco, arriving by 9 a.m. local time. There we connected with another friend and drove down to Sand Hill Road in Palo Alto for appointments with three different venture capital firms.

For those who don't know Palo Alto or Sand Hill Road, it is an area renowned for starting some of the largest companies in the world. Think Wall Street for start-up companies. If you are using something technological today, chances are that the genesis of the product happened on Sand Hill Road. The same could be said for several medical products and revolutionary energy products. Many billionaires either work on Sand Hill Road or were first funded there.

So here we were, three average guys peddling a five-page business plan, asking for $2 million to start our new company. Because I had worked only in corporate America up to that point, the thought of what we were asking seemed outrageous. In most corporations, gaining access to just $10,000 requires three levels of approval, a detailed business plan, and about six months. That we would be so bold as to request $2 million was beyond my comprehension.

When we arrived at the compound of office suites, I was more than a little nervous. I felt somewhat embarrassed to be there and was certain that we would be summarily rejected. The office complex sprawled across many acres, and I could not quite get my arms around the fact that billions upon billions of dollars were being invested every week from this very location.

We entered the conference room for our first appointment and waited quite a while. I had been up for about ten hours by this point, so my energy level had already peaked and waned about thirty times since I had first opened my eyes that morning. The long wait lulled me into a meditative, sleepy state, and I was concerned that I would not have a good energy level when the time came.

The three of us had already decided that, given my background, I would be CEO of the new company. Therefore, while all of us would be part of the presentation that day, it would be my role to set the tone of our session. I felt completely inadequate for the task. I thought that my insecurity about the whole issue was like a flashing neon sign saying, "Do not invest in our company!"

Finally, the eight partners and analysts of the venture capital firm made their way into the conference room. They were pleasant, but they also had an air about them that silently declared, "We have billions, and you don't. We have entrepreneurs come to us every day asking for money. They all think that their ideas are brilliant, but most of them are not. We are skeptical of every conversation and only invest in one company in every fifty that come into our office. We'll be polite just in case you are one of those fifty, but we really think you are wasting our time. Now let's get started."

The Long Silence

I don't remember who spoke first or how long we were there. I only remember that I spoke last. I thought that my finish was pretty strong, but when I stopped speaking there was no visible reaction from the investors around the table. Nothing. The silence lasted maybe a minute, but it felt like an hour.

Awkward.

My mind raced. *See, I told you this was foolish. Who in their right mind would give you a couple million dollars? It's better just to stay where you are, comfortable in a place where you can care for your family. You've got a huge payday coming, so just hold on for the big money. It's a sure thing, whereas this route is filled with risk and stress. You really didn't want this money anyway.*

With those thoughts pounding through my mind, the pressure of the long silence lessened. My friends and I knew that in negotiating there comes a time when you should just shut up and literally not say a word. We allowed the silence to fill the room. Seven of the eight avoided eye contact by looking down at their papers on the table. Then finally they cast their eyes on the eighth man, the senior partner at the table.

When it became clear that he would be the first to speak, he leaned over the table and cleared his throat. "If you promise not to go to your next appointment," he said, "we'll give you $10 million to start your company."

Say what? They not only liked our idea—they wanted to expand on the business concept and give us five times what we were asking. How could that be possible?

I started to accept the offer, but one of my friends wisely and diplomatically declined. He thanked them and indicated that we would keep the rest of our appointments that day. My friend knew that these potential investors were offering more money in exchange for a larger share of the ownership of our company, which would limit our ability to control the concept. I was grateful to have had two friends with me who were much wiser and more mature.

We finished our last appointment around 7 p.m. The last group of investors offered the $2 million we were requesting, and they felt right to us culturally, so we returned to the hotel and worked on a term sheet until midnight—almost twenty-four hours after I'd gotten up to begin this wild adventure. Although I was exhausted, it had been one of the most exciting days of my life.

But my excitement quickly faded upon returning home.

Walking a Wobbly Wire

The following morning, I found my wife, Deborah, sitting up in bed, crying over my decision to leave the security of corporate life. Our daughter required extensive medical care—how could I be so selfish as to want a job that didn't guarantee she would be cared for? How could I want something that would put the entire family at risk?

And Deborah was right. My motives for leaving my relatively secure job were completely self-centered. I was tired of the corporate life and wanted the experience of breaking out on my own. I wanted to build something from the ground up, in which my success or failure would be completely my own responsibility. I wanted to create something positive rather than always focusing on the tough task of rebuilding something that somebody else owned. I wanted to play with the big boys in the tech industry.

I wanted, I wanted, I wanted. My restlessness had nothing to do with what my family needed or with what God wanted for my life.

But my friends and I were too far down the rabbit hole to stop now, so we proceeded with the plan. The following two years were everything you might expect from a start-up company. There were thrilling moments and tough moments. Much of the work gave us the incredible freedom to be creative and entrepreneurial, while that same freedom brought intense pressures to meet deadlines and make payroll. We averaged twenty-hour days on the job, and the four hours spent sleeping went more like a series of occasional naps.

We walked a wobbly wire between survival and shutdown, which was both exhilarating and stressful. One weekend, Deborah and I hosted a party for my associates at our house. People brought their spouses and children, and almost everybody was having a great time . . . except for me. I retreated to my bedroom and looked out at the fifty or so families playing in the backyard.

This party was on a Saturday, and I had no idea how we were going to make payroll the following Friday. I was about to let down literally hundreds of good people. As I watched these people talk, laugh, and play together in my yard, I began to pine for the days of corporate America and the sense of security it offered. I had wanted to escape the confines of rules, authority, and policy, but those things seemed so comfortable to me now—I just hadn't seen it at the time. Now I was faced with leadership challenges that were choking me all the more.

I prayed for forgiveness for my arrogance. While I had left my last job for selfish reasons, I asked God to bless our new venture despite my self-centeredness. God knew that I would ultimately pray that prayer, and he stepped in to save my bacon. I also now believe that he was the drive behind me wanting to leave the safety of corporate America in the first place. He knew that I needed to learn this lesson as an important part of my growth. We made payroll that Friday, and ultimately our business became very successful.

Our company is now known beyond the USA and is highly profitable. It became the largest company of its kind in less than three years with more than $6 billion in volume. The technology we created has saved our customers tens of millions of dollars. It still excites me to see it so abundantly successful. Our investors are happy, and the company that ultimately bought our business is happy too.

God had used this journey to show me an important lesson about valuing the position in which he has placed me. It was also a lesson about seeing the consequences of leaving before his appointed time and for reasons other than his will for me. In the process, he also showed me that *when it suits his purpose*, there is a time to leave the safety and security of our current position to grow beyond where we are at the moment.

A Perpetual State of "What Else?"

Sometimes God wants us to stay where we are in life, and sometimes he wants us to step up to the precipice and make a leap despite the risks and the naysayers. Sometimes he wants us to follow our passion, and sometimes he wants us to learn the lessons offered by staying right where we are.

The real challenge for you and me is to discern the difference between the two.

For all of us who identify ourselves as followers of Christ, our obligation is to avoid jumping across the precipice just because we long to escape our current circumstances or because it happens to feel right or exciting at the time. Rather, our job is to put our selfish excuses aside and listen for what God is up to in our current situation. We need to pause, pray, listen, and hear what God truly wants us to do. It may be that he in fact has plans for us to do something else somewhere else. But I would speculate that it's far more likely that God wants most of us to stay where we are, at least for now, instead of jumping ship.

God has placed you, me, and the rest of his children where we are for a specific reason and purpose. Until we make the most of what he's given us and fulfill that purpose, it's likely that anywhere else we move will be overflowing with problems similar to what we experienced before we left. What character-building lesson does God want you to learn where you are today? What lessons in spiritual growth does he have in store for you where you are? I've learned (often the hard way) that when we try to escape what God has planned for us, he'll only increase the volume on those lessons until we hear him. (Think Jonah and the big fish.) If we leap before we are ready, he'll make sure that the same lessons show up wherever we go!

I'm also convinced that God looks for us to be grateful for what we have before he brings new things into our lives. His Word says, "Be joyful always; pray continually; give thanks in all circumstances, for this is God's will for you in Christ Jesus" (1 Thessalonians 5:16-18). Yet many of us live in a perpetual state of asking, "What else?"—wanting, waiting, and praying for the next promotion, the next offer, the next opportunity because, after all, *It must be better than where we are now.* We consume far too much time and energy longing for "something better" to happen instead of being thankful for what is right before our eyes.

And that was me! When things were going well in my career, I was always thinking about what was next. When will I be promoted? When will people realize that I'm as good as I think I am? When will I make more money? When will I get to be CEO? When will I move beyond this boring job and do something more exciting?

Of course, the next job would be exciting for a time—but soon I would find myself asking the same questions. No matter what I had, it wasn't enough. No matter how good things were, they weren't good enough. And if there was any problem at work, it was as though the world had placed this huge burden on me and left me to deal with it all by myself. Poor Scott—such a tough life!

But with the help of some great mentors, I finally began to ask myself some better questions. These were positive, constructive questions like "What if I could turn this around?" and "What if I could see that the job is only the vehicle God has given me to grow into my faith, honor him, and serve other people?" If I could see that, I might not be so bored, frustrated, or ready to look for the "what else?" to fulfill me.

In his first letter to the Corinthians, the apostle Paul addressed this very idea. He recognized the human desire to change our circumstances, but the essence of his message is that we should continue down whatever path God has placed us on. If we are single, we should be content with being single. If we are married, we should stay married. He even goes so far as to say that if we are slaves, we should be faithful slaves. How's that for staying in a tough work environment?

As long as we are not living in immorality, the apostle wrote, we are to please God by being content in whatever life situation he has placed us: "Each one should remain in the situation which he was in when God called him" (1 Corinthians 7:20).

A very rich man once visited Mother Teresa as she ministered in the slums of Calcutta. Overcome by the scenes of poverty and despair, the man asked if he should stay there to help. Her response? "Grow where you are planted." In other words, "There is work to be done in your current circumstances back home. Go do God's work there. You have been placed there for a reason. Go find out what God has in store where he planted you."

And this is the message I received in my basement back in 2002 when I finally took the time to pray, sit quietly, and listen for God's guidance. My heavenly Father was essentially telling me, "Stop looking for me outside of your work. I am not separate from your work. I am in your work. You don't have to leave work to serve me. I am part of you wherever you are. There are people at work I want you to serve. There are things at work I want you to do. Work is where I will serve you, and it will be the platform from which I will serve others through you."

Although it has taken many years for me to see it come to pass, this is exactly what he has done. It was through work that I met the people who would ultimately show me what it really means to love the Lord. It was where I would come to experience love, forgiveness, and unconditional support during a very difficult time in my personal life. It was there that I met people who would ultimately allow this book to be written and published. And it was there that I learned to go about business in a way that I hope is far more pleasing to God.

Settle In Before Branching Out

I recognize that while some readers have found their calling at work, many others are weary with their jobs. You might be among the latter group—bored, frustrated, unfulfilled, longing for something different and more exciting or more in alignment with your spiritual calling. I've been there too. I've felt what you're feeling, and I've thought what you're thinking. My advice to you is to pray about this biblical principle: *Until you deal with any unresolved spiritual issues, it will not matter what job opportunity you move to.* The same issues will follow you wherever you go. In fact, they're likely to be worse.

Deal with those issues where you are. Be the best employee, the best coworker, and the best person where you are. Make the most of what you have now. Become who God wants you to be — where you are. Don't even contemplate moving on until you've discovered the joy of peace and contentment with your present circumstances.

In Matthew 12:44, Jesus talked about how an evil spirit, once rejected from a household, will wander for a while and then come back to the place he once lived. If the house is found empty, the evil spirit will not only return, but he will also bring his friends with him. In other words, if the person (the house) is swept clean but does not then consistently tend to the house (repent, abide, obey), then even worse things will come to him.

You might have seen this happen with a friend or family member or even in your own life. You move clear across the country to get a fresh start only to find that the same problems haunt you — sometimes with greater intensity than before. It can happen when moving into a new locale, a new school, a new job, or with a new spouse. *If we don't change on the inside, it doesn't matter what we change on the outside.* We will create and experience the same problems again and again. We might change our address, but we won't change who we are.

This is not to say that we should never journey to a new place to achieve spiritual growth. Sometimes we need to be repotted to allow our roots to grow or be moved into the sun so we can flourish. God has called many of his people to leave their comfortable surroundings to follow him into new circumstances. Examples abound, including Noah, Abraham, and Moses. Most of these people objected, sometimes strenuously, to making a change. It was not they who wanted to move but rather God who wanted to replant them.

Conversely, if *we* are the ones looking to grow into some other life situation, we have to make sure that we have honestly examined our motives. Are we leaving because we are bored, frustrated, or discouraged? Are we leaving to escape a problem or conflict? Are we feeling underappreciated or underpaid? Are we feeling put-upon or discriminated against? Are we feeling ignored or like a number in a nameless sea of employees?

If we truly trust God to make his way clear, then we need to settle back regardless of our current circumstances. We need to trust that he will surround us with the right people at the right time in the right situations to allow his path for us to become clear. It means that we stay alert, present, and enthusiastic about what unfolds before us over time—loyal to our employers, diligent in our jobs, and positive and affirming among our coworkers. God can fix anything if we give him the space to do it his way and according to his timetable.

If we trust that God has put us in our present surroundings for a reason, then that reason will unfold before us when he knows that the time is right. Eventually, it might become clear that it's time to move somewhere else. But we might also see a new, higher purpose for staying right where we are. We might finally understand why God has us where he has us, embrace his loving sovereignty and provision, and grow where we are planted.

And when we open our hearts to God's purpose, we just might stop waiting for someone or something else to make us happy. Our contentment and enthusiasm will come from a place much deeper inside. Our fulfillment will come from a place of service rather than from the particular job we are in at the moment. We will stop waiting and longing for a change to make us happy and be happy with what we have.

If we are truly grateful for what we have and where we are, we will treat the present situation with respect and admiration. When we are grateful for our current job, we will bring a heightened sense of purpose to it every day. We will work with authentic passion and produce greater results. When we produce greater results, we will be serving our people, our customers, and our company much more vigorously than we did before. When people see this in us, we will often be recognized, promoted, and paid more, even though that's not what we set out to do.

Conversely, if we are ungrateful, we will become like a cancer in an organization and then wonder why no one appreciates us.

So until the time comes when God clearly moves you into a new pot so that your roots can dig deeper and your branches spread farther, bloom and grow where you are planted. Draw on the strength of God's Holy Spirit within you, and be a blessing to your coworkers, your boss, your customers, and your organization. Make each day the very best work you've ever done. When you abide in the Vine, the life that flows through you will change you and those around you. Find God in your present job before you seek him in a new one. Once you find him, you just might discover that you can branch out right where you are.

For Reflection and Discussion

1. Do you view your work as just a job? How might it also be a ministry?
2. What might God want to accomplish through you at your current workplace?
3. Are you so focused on your career that you've never even thought about what God might want to do through you at work?
4. If you are not living your passion, should you change careers?
5. What if your seemingly difficult boss needs encouragement and needs someone to show him or her a path to God?
6. What if you were the only Christian in an organization filled with unbelievers? Are you trapped in that case, or are you a bright, shining light? Are you the only example of Christ that your coworkers might ever see?
7. If you are thinking about telling your company to "take this job and shove it," is such an attitude really more about your company or you?
8. If you are looking to change jobs, have you prayed about whether that is what God wants for you?
9. Do you think it's possible that God could change your circumstances at work? Could he make them better? Could he change the

people you work with? Could he change you and your perspective on your work environment?

10. If you took your workplace problems to God, how would you describe them? Write that down. Now look at what you just wrote. Is it more about you or more about how you could serve God?

Preparation for the Week Ahead

Keep track of your thoughts this coming week. How much time do you spend thinking, "What else?"

How much time do you spend wishing you had something other than what you actually have? How much time do you spend thinking that you'll be happy when some other "big thing" happens?

Now notice what happens when you release these thoughts and allow yourself the space to see what God might be up to in your life right now. Does it change your perspective at all?

A Prayer for the Week Ahead

Father, I seek your guidance this week to help me discern what you want for me in my working life. Do you want me to stay where I am and discover a new purpose for my present work situation, or do you want me to follow you to a new destination, trusting that you will be with me no matter how risky that path may appear?

While I wait for your answer, I will lay aside my personal agenda and seek only your wisdom. I won't feel pressure to know now. I will relax in the knowledge that your timing is perfect. I won't try to force conversations or manipulate my daily walk. I will wait patiently and expectantly, and meanwhile I will remain fully faithful to my present duties as well as to my coworkers, my boss, and my company, for "whatever [I] do, whether in word or deed, [I will] do it all in the name of the Lord Jesus" (Colossians 3:17).

I know that you reveal yourself to those who abide in your will. And so I will abide in Christ, enjoying by faith his protection and love for me.

I won't pray for anything specific to happen. I will leave room for you to respond in a way that I could never imagine on my own. I will simply wait on you so that I might know your will for me at work, wherever that truth might lead me.

I pray all of this in Jesus' name. Amen.

2

That'll Leave a Mark

PRINCIPLE 2: *Serve others more than self.*

So the last will be first, and the first will be last.

— MATTHEW 20:16

Do nothing out of selfish ambition or vain conceit, but in humility consider others better than yourselves. Each of you should look not only to your own interests, but also to the interests of others.

— PHILIPPIANS 2:3-4

Everyone has a boss. We learn from our boss things that we would want to emulate as well as things that we would never want to do to other people. I've been blessed to have great bosses throughout my career. They have been helpful, caring, intelligent, and supportive. Many of them cared more about me than they cared about their own performance. But as great as my bosses have been to me, I haven't always been that kind of boss to other people.

I remember my first work assignment out of college, in which I was given the honor of having other people report to me. Unfortunately, I was too young and immature to view leadership as a privilege — as something to care for and respect. Instead, I thought it was cool to be someone's boss and treated the position as a right rather than as an honor to be treasured.

After only three months of training in my first job ever, I was named manager of a 300,000-foot distribution center with about fifty employees reporting to me. I had never driven a truck but would be responsible for fifteen big rig drivers. I'd never driven a forklift but was given responsibility for twenty-five order pickers. I'd never supervised a manufacturing plant but would oversee ten package assembly employees. What a rush! People with more than thirty years on the job would now report to me.

Then I showed up to my first day of work. The team barely said hello. No one looked to me for direction, which was fine because I didn't know what I was doing anyway. I walked from place to place feeling as awkward as I'm sure I looked. It was one of the most uncomfortable days of my career. My job title and my company told me I had power, but in the eyes of the people who reported to me I had none.

While that should have humbled me, it did not. It only strengthened my resolve. I worked harder. I got dirtier. I talked to people even when they did not talk to me. I did performance reviews even though I'm sure that no one listened to my feedback. I did all the things my mind told me to do in order to earn the respect of my employees. But when the time came for me to move on to my next assignment, I did not get the warm send-off I had hoped for at my promotion celebration. Instead, I received a very different kind of message from one of the big rig drivers. His name was Chuck.

Thirty years later, I can still picture the room we were in, what Chuck was wearing, where other people were sitting, and how they reacted to the conversation. While everyone else was at least polite to me during this dinner party, Chuck took me to task. In front of my boss, Chuck told me that I had provided no leadership and that the team had little respect for me. Even if I was being promoted to the next level, I was worthless in his eyes. Chuck was glad to see me go.

Ouch! That'll Leave a Mark

I had gotten my first leadership assignment all wrong. My goal during those two years had been to earn my team's respect as their boss — but not as their leader. I got dirty but only to understand their job better so that I could tell them what to do. I worked triple shifts but only to demonstrate that I could be one of the guys and work their jobs harder than they could. I brought them food and helped them to get things done but only so that they would perform better.

I was doing everything I could to earn the right to have power over them, but I didn't do anything for them as my coworkers. I was nice to them, but I did not actually care for them. I only wanted them to produce the results I needed in order to get promoted. They sensed this in me. And while our work relationship had improved over time as they saw me willing to put in the effort, our leadership relationship was reversed: They produced results in spite of me, not because of me. They worked around me rather than with me. They simply waited me out.

Chuck was right. As painful as his commentary was that evening, he taught me more about life than I ever would have learned without him. By being brutally honest, he provided me with more leadership in that one encounter than I had shown him in two years. I don't think Chuck intended to help me that night, but his comments showed me what it really means to lead a team. He was strong enough to show me the negative implications of my self-centered approach to management.

While it took me many years and more Chuck-like lessons, I finally realized that if I could have a negative impact on my coworkers, I could also have a positive impact. It was possible to reverse the paradigm, but it would require a shift in my perspective. I had already learned that I couldn't fake my way to sincerity. In order for me to be effective, sincerity had to come from somewhere inside me.

But as a hard-charging manager who still did not completely trust in God's goodness, I needed proof. I was in the secular world, and I needed some secular evidence that if I made a change to an others-first approach, I'd produce at least the same results as when I put myself first.

As it turns out, validation could be found in both secular and spiritual texts. The world and God's Word actually agree that a selfless, more humble approach to the workplace produces better outcomes. Let's start with the secular perspective.

The Secular View

Prior to 1960, the overriding managerial philosophy was based on something known as Theory X, which is a belief that workers are inherently lazy and must be manipulated to productivity through rewards and punishments. During the 1960s, Theory Y began to emerge, contending that workers require self-actualization, the socio-emotional human need that Abraham Maslow placed at the top of his famous hierarchy of needs. Theory Y postulated that simply telling a worker what to do does not help him self-actualize. He needs to connect with something larger than himself and find significance in it in order to reach his full potential.

In the 1970s, Robert Greenleaf coined the phrase "servant leadership" in his similarly titled book. Greenleaf cited examples of successful leadership in which company executives managed as though they were there to serve their employees and not the other way around.

In the 1980s, Stephen Covey built on the philosophy of servant leadership in his best-selling book *The 7 Habits of Highly Effective People*. His habits, such as "Seek first to understand, then to be understood," were conducive to serving other people before serving yourself. Covey credits Greenleaf's *Servant Leadership* as one of his inspirations.

In the 1990s, a book titled *Emotional Intelligence* by Daniel Goleman discussed the concept that people and organizations must address both right-brain and left-brain needs. While left-brain proclivities tend to be more pragmatic, dictatorial, and logical, right-brain needs are more creative, spiritual, and emotional. Goleman contended that the most effective leaders and the most productive organizations attend to both the logical *and* emotional needs of their culture.

In 2001, one of the best-selling business books of all time was published. *Good to Great*, by Jim Collins, devoted an entire chapter to what Collins called "Level 5 leaders." While these leaders are passionately focused on their organization's mission, they are also humble and quiet and prefer to let their people shine rather than take personal credit for company performance. Level 5 leaders produce the best global results that are sustainable over time. This is not theory, Collins found, but fact. *Leaders who place their companies and their people ahead of themselves are simply more successful than self-absorbed, egotistical, greedy leaders.*

When you let that sink in, it really does make sense. A leader who places the needs of her people ahead of her own will nurture an intense loyalty among her workforce. She will attract other servant-leaders who will put their own team ahead of themselves throughout the entire organization. The team will seek solutions without regard for personal gain. The needs of the company will always be placed ahead of the needs of any one individual, yet meeting the needs of the individual is what creates that culture in the first place. It's a virtuous circle.

My intellectual curiosity was satisfied. I could see how putting others ahead of self could build a better company and produce better results over the long term. Yet I was still not sure that there was any spiritual data to verify the point. I knew that the Bible was filled with commentary about service to humanity but was there any proof that it actually leads to better results? After all, I work for a secular company, and results are what I'm paid for.

The Spiritual View

In Acts 20:35, we are reminded that Jesus said, "It is more blessed to give than to receive." But without a spiritual perspective, that statement sounds like a platitude—you know, the kind of sentiment that people are supposed to believe in but no one really does.

As a kid, it was virtually impossible for me to grasp such a concept. How is it possible that it's better to give stuff than to get stuff? It made no sense whatsoever. It's way cooler to get stuff than to give stuff.

So if it felt that way as a child, how could it be that giving of myself would produce better results at work?

God and His Word tend to be highly counterintuitive. And the Bible clearly articulates a simple law of sowing and reaping that appears repeatedly throughout both the Old Testament and the New Testament. Also called the law of reciprocity, this rule helps us understand that whatever we invest in terms of money, love, time, effort, mercy, forgiveness, or support is what we will receive in return from God.

For example, in Matthew 18:23-35 we learn a lesson about how the law of sowing and reaping works in banking. A king wanted to settle accounts with people who owed him money. One man was brought before him and was ordered to pay up or go to prison. He begged for more time to pay. The king was so moved by his plea that he forgave the man's debt entirely.

But no sooner was the man out of the king's castle when he saw someone who owed him far less money than he himself had owed the king. He cornered the debtor and demanded his money. The debtor pleaded for more time, but the man refused to grant either time or forgiveness. In fact, he beat the debtor and had him thrown into prison.

When the king's servants witnessed this act, the man whose debt had been forgiven was once again brought before the king. The king told him that because he had shown no mercy, the king would in turn have no mercy on him. The man was sent to prison and tortured for his debts.

This parable teaches that we will receive whatever we dish out. In fact, in telling this story Jesus goes so far as to say that this is what "the kingdom of heaven is like." Jesus specifically says that God and his kingdom work this way. Just as the law of gravity is a natural law of God's created earth, so the law of reciprocity is a spiritual law of the kingdom of heaven. Jesus didn't say, "This is how you should act" or "Maybe this will happen if you act right." He said, in essence, "This is how it is—how the Father designed it."

God gives to us whatever we give to other people. If we are selfish, greedy, hateful, or manipulative, that is how God will cause other people to act around us. But, thank God, the law of sowing and reaping also works in the positive sense. And this is what Jesus wanted his followers to grasp. If we are forgiving, helpful, kind, and generous, then that is what will be shown to us. So, as we seek to put God to work, if you and I place the needs of others ahead of our own needs, even our customers will act less selfishly around us. They will place our needs ahead of their own needs. God will send to us whatever we have sent out into the world.

Throughout the Bible, we see further validation that God will heap blessings on us when we put the needs of other people ahead of our own needs. Consider the following Scripture passages carefully. Ask God to open your eyes and your heart to their underlying message. Also, ask how you might apply these promises to your challenges and relationships at work during the coming weeks.

Give, and it will be given to you. A good measure, pressed down, shaken together and running over, will be poured into your lap. (Luke 6:38)

Remember this: Whoever sows sparingly will also reap sparingly, and whoever sows generously will also reap generously. (2 Corinthians 9:6)

Sow for yourselves righteousness, reap the fruit of unfailing love. (Hosea 10:12)

A man reaps what he sows. The one who sows to please his sinful nature, from that nature will reap destruction; the one who sows to please the Spirit, from the Spirit will reap eternal life. Let us not become weary in doing good, for at the proper time we will reap a harvest if we do not give up. Therefore, as we have opportunity, let us do good to all people. (Galatians 6:7-10)

You know that the rulers of the Gentiles lord it over them, and their high officials exercise authority over them. Not so with you. Instead, whoever wants to become great among you must be your servant, and whoever wants to be first must be your slave—just as the Son of Man did not come to be served, but to serve, and to give his life as a ransom for many. (Matthew 20:25-28)

Test me in this . . . and see if I will not throw open the floodgates of heaven and pour out so much blessing that you will not have room enough for it. I will prevent pests from devouring your crops, and the vines in your fields will not cast their fruit. . . . Then all the nations will call you blessed, for yours will be a delightful land. (Malachi 3:10-12)

If, guided by God's Holy Spirit, we place the needs of others before our own, God will use our life circumstances to pour blessings on us. Conversely, if we follow our sinful nature and use people and take from them, God will use people and events to cause our own destruction. Time after time, the Bible tells us that whatever we give is what we will get. If we want love, we must be loving. If we want respect, we must show respect. If we want money, we must give money away. If we want power, we must entrust other people with power. If we want to be successful, we must make sure that the people around us are successful. So when it comes to being an effective leader at work, *the best way to ensure our own abundance is to make sure we are putting the abundance of our organization and our people ahead of our own.*

Not everyone reading this book is a manager of people, but that should not impact how you relate to this principle. Placing others ahead of self is a *life* principle, not just a *work* principle. A life of service to others makes a difference in how you interact with your family, your church, your friends, and your coworkers. It will positively impact how you relate to your boss, your spouse, and your children. It will make you a better leader at home, in your community, and in your workplace. It is through such counterintuitive, humble, others-before-self leadership that we will produce more for and with the people we serve — even if those people do not officially report to us.

God goes to work with us when we humble ourselves before him and others and place others ahead of ourselves. For those who rely on their own sense of power, God lets them play the power game, which is fickle at best. But for those who empty themselves and entrust their daily lives to his control, he rushes in to fill the space. When we look to give to others, he not only provides what we ask, but he also gives abundantly so that we can be generous in our giving.

In my career, I have found that the more I give to my people, the more I seem to receive in return. Whether it's bonuses or benefits or raises or praise, the more that I'm able to pass along to the people in the business, the better they take care of our customers and the better our customers take care of us. Conversely, whenever I've scrimped, the business has suffered and so has my own personal reward and satisfaction.

It Begins and Ends with Chuck

So let's wrap up this principle by going back to my story about Chuck. I only wish that I had actually learned Chuck's lesson on that night when he spoke to me so sternly. Instead, I just worked that much harder to be a stronger (not better) boss. I became more dictatorial about what needed to be done. No one would put me aside again (or at least as far as I could tell). People would know who was in charge and do what I said. I was kind, but I was also very firm in my approach.

It would take me several more years to get what Chuck had tried to tell me. Today, almost thirty years later, I'm still learning Chuck's lesson. But now I am able to put some of it into action. Rather than manipulate my team, I frequently pray for them. I don't pray for their performance; I pray for *them*. I pray that they may be fulfilled and joyful in life and at work.

I pray to see how I can best serve and support them. I pray that their families thrive and that their sense of purpose is realized. I pray for their well-being and for their career. When they are working on tough assignments, I pray that they might be able to know themselves better as leaders and as people. I no longer think of them as a means to my success. I think of them as people I care about and for whom I have a great responsibility.

I don't know if they feel my prayer or not, but that's not the point. The point is the work that is done in me and in them when I bring God into the relationship. I'm not exactly the warm and fuzzy type. I don't claim to be my people's best friend. But I do know that my main concern is for their well-being and success in life. I truly want to help them develop into the best possible leaders they can be and to learn about themselves in the process.

We can bring God into our workplace by doing as he has commanded us to do. When we put others in front of ourselves, we will see how quickly our results begin to flourish. It might take some time to create a cultural shift, but we shouldn't let that discourage us. It takes only one person to change the world. Imagine how much we can change just within our organizations. Whether we are a CEO or a frontline associate, we can change the entire tone of our workplace by living this principle. Putting others ahead of self will end up making us more successful than we can imagine.

For Reflection and Discussion

1. Is the law of sowing and reaping (aka the law of reciprocity) really true? How have you seen this principle work in and around your life?
2. Whether you are very nice to those around you or very harsh, what are your real motives with your coworkers?
3. Has there been a Chuck in your career? What message was that person trying to send you?
4. Why do some people get results even though they act contrary to God's Word?
5. Do you think that it's possible to advance your career by helping other people advance their careers?
6. Are you trying to advance your career, or are you trying to advance God's kingdom?
7. In your workplace, in what ways would putting others first really lead to better results?

8. Why has God placed you at your company or organization? Is there someone or some group of people there whom you might have been sent to serve?

9. What are some examples of companies you have seen that put their people first? How are they successful?

10. Do nice guys finish first or last?

11. Does the biblical view of serving others agree or disagree with the secular business view of how to treat associates?

12. How can you win company competitions if you are serving the very people you are competing against?

Preparation for the Week Ahead

Note your behavior during the next week. How often do you act out of self-interest rather than the interests of others? Include in this observation whom you speak with, what you think about, where you spend your money, and where you spend your time.

Try serving others first for a month. In every action, think about whether what you are doing is to your advantage or to another's advantage. See what God does in your life when you take this approach. Watch how other people respond to you.

A Prayer for the Week Ahead

Father, I acknowledge that my first thought is almost always about myself. I repent of that self-centeredness and ask that you plant in me a heart that seeks to serve rather than to be served. Help me to see even the small things I do that are aimed at making my own life better above and beyond those around me. Help me to lead with a servant's heart and be respectful and humble to those both above and below my rank. It is in Christ's name that I pray. Amen.

3

It's Reigning Cats and Dogs

PRINCIPLE 3: *Humility is the first and most important ingredient.*

Humility and the fear of the LORD bring wealth and honor and life.
— PROVERBS 22:4

Humble yourselves before the Lord, and he will lift you up.
— JAMES 4:10

He guides the humble in what is right and teaches them his way.
— PSALM 25:9

I love dogs. I've had them all my life. I know how they act, what they like, and how they think. Our dogs have always been off-leash trained, loyal, and happy. At the moment, we have only one dog, whose name is Max. But this year my daughter also brought a cat into our house. She named the cat Bailey. What an adjustment! Not only does Max appear to be asking, "What have you done?" but my wife and I are at a loss to figure out how to deal with this new personality in our house.

My sister sent me something on the Internet to help me adjust. (The source is anonymous.) It's a comical depiction of how a dog might write a diary as compared to a cat doing the same thing. The fictional dog's diary entries speak of how life is so great. He writes about how he got breakfast—his favorite thing. Then he got to go on a walk—his favorite thing. And then he got to ride in the car—once again, his favorite thing. And so on throughout the day.

The cat diary begins with "Day 765 of My Captivity." The cat goes on to talk about how his captors taunt him with dangling objects. He tries to kill them by walking about their feet on the stairs. At one point he brings home a decapitated mouse to "show them what I'm capable of."

It's a very funny and somewhat accurate depiction of how dogs act versus cats. It reminds me of another dog-cat reference I heard years ago from the book *Cat and Dog Theology* by Bob Sjogren and Gerald Robison. (I strongly recommend this book.) To paraphrase, dog theology goes like this: "My owner feeds me, cares for me, cleans up after me, and plays with me. My owner must be God." Cat theology, on the other hand, goes like this: "My owner feeds me, cares for me, cleans up after me, and plays with me. *I* must be God."

What a difference in thinking! One theology says it's all about my master, while the other says it's all about me. One theology says I'll follow my master wherever he goes. The other says I'll deal with my owner when I want and where I want. Dog theology states that my master knows better than me and provides what is best for me. Cat theology believes that my owner is here to do my bidding because I am the master of my life. One theology is based on humility, and the other is based on arrogance.

Now, to give Bailey credit, she's a great cat. While I wouldn't yet describe myself as a cat person, I'm coming around to accepting cats as something more than just totally selfish little creatures. Yet the dog-cat comparison is a great picture of how many of us think about God. If we're honest about our relationship with him, we'll have to admit that we tend to behave more like Bailey than Max. Our relationship with God tends to be on our terms, in our timing, and for our convenience. It's all about *us*.

That has certainly been true for me. I used to regard God as I would a genie in a bottle. I let him out when it served my interests and when I needed him to fulfill my wishes. If he didn't succumb to my every whim, then back in the bottle he went. What use was God if he wasn't going to make things happen for me? What good was God if he wasn't prepared to meet me on my terms and timeline?

I also have to admit that I've acted more like Bailey toward people. I would show up when I wanted to, do what I wanted once I got there, and do only what I was interested in doing—nothing more. I'm proud, stubborn, and confident in my own abilities. Why would I need to listen to anyone else, follow their direction, or do what they ask me to do? Why should I listen to my parents, my wife, or my children? After all, I'm an adult now, and I'm the spiritual leader of my home. I'm the one in charge, not them.

How's that for ego? How's that for the surest and quickest path to having everyone around me reach the quick conclusion that I'm arrogant and completely disinterested in anything they have to say? As a result of my attitude, people would either shut down around me to avoid conflict, or they would get aggressive to try to break through my egotistical fortress. Neither response was good for them, for me, or for my company.

In addition to alienating my coworkers, an arrogant, me-first approach to life ensures that God will not be present in my work. When I focus on worldly things like ego, power, or status, God grants me the freedom to head down that path of self-destruction. He quietly tells me that if I think I know better than he does, then I should definitely take my own advice. He leaves me free to do what I will and therefore accept the consequences of whatever I do.

Sometimes those consequences will be good, and sometimes they will be bad. But without fail, the consequences will be based on the fickle fate of the world. Without humility, we shut off access to God's wisdom, creativity, guidance, and abundance. We are left to our own devices, hard work, and cleverness—all of which pale in comparison to the strength and power that come from God.

Humility Changes Everything

One of the best examples of how humility can lead to greater success is my friend Andrew, who was the top salesperson in his company while he was still in corporate America. Andrew just might have been the best in his industry. His company is a multinational, multibillion-dollar business, and Andrew produced the best results for them anywhere. If they wanted to train a salesperson, they sent that rep to Andrew. If they had a difficult account, they'd give it to Andrew. If they wanted input into a product or service, they would ask Andrew for his opinion.

What people could not figure out was how Andrew produced such incredible results. Accounts that would not produce anything for decades would suddenly flourish when Andrew took them over. When problems occurred, they seemed not to affect Andrew's territory as badly as they did other parts of the world. It just seemed that Andrew had the magic touch.

Indeed he did.

Andrew prayed for his customers. He prayed for their success. He prayed for the Holy Spirit to open their hearts to God. He prayed for success in his business but mostly that his customers would be successful in *their* business.

Andrew would ask God to show him how he could serve others in his business and how he should respond to particular clients or difficult situations.

Andrew told me about one exceptionally nasty customer whom nobody could crack. Naturally, Andrew's company gave the account to him. He went to see this client for an appointment, and the person would not come out to see him. At one point, the client walked right past Andrew and went out to lunch. On his way out, he asked Andrew, "What are you doing here?" and didn't even pause for a response. Andrew just waited for him to return.

After returning, the client finally called my friend into his office. He cussed him out and barked orders at him. Andrew just sat there and took the heat. The client took phone calls in the middle of their meeting. Andrew just sat there.

Finally, Andrew said, "I can see that you're very busy and that this isn't the best time for you. I want to respect your time, so I'll come back when it's more convenient." But the client kept on berating him. Andrew looked down and saw his customer's sandwich only half-eaten. "You haven't even had time for lunch. I can't imagine how busy you are and how much pressure you must be under. I don't want to be one more burden to you. I'll just come back when I can be more helpful with your schedule." Andrew was not asking to leave because he wanted to leave. He sincerely thought his presence was not in his customer's best interest at that moment in time.

But the client kept ranting. My friend then stood and said, "I have so much respect for you that I can't take any more of your time today. It's clear that I've come at an inconvenient time. I just want to be helpful, and that's not what's happening today. I'll work with your assistant to set up an appointment for a time when people aren't coming at you so fast."

With that, the customer softened. He apologized and asked Andrew to sit. They talked for another forty-five minutes about things that had nothing to do with business. During that time, Andrew demonstrated that he cared more about the customer than about whatever business he might pick up that day. But by the end of visit, he walked out with a big order. Within months, this client's business became one of Andrew's best accounts.

My friend demonstrated humility many times during that encounter. He could have walked out of that office when the client didn't meet with him on time, and he could have walked out any number of times while he was being scolded and berated. Andrew demonstrated humility when he cared more about what was happening in his customer's life than about what business he might pick up. He put his pride on hold while the customer vented.

Some people would call Andrew lucky with the business he acquired at this account. I'd call it God exalting Andrew for being Christlike with a difficult customer. How many of us would have walked out or, worse, fired back with something that would have burned bridges forever?

Humility Is the First Step

The Bible tells us in Matthew 23:12, "Whoever exalts himself will be humbled, and whoever humbles himself will be exalted." God lifts up those who humble themselves, but on those who are arrogant he brings forces to bear that are very likely to *cause* humility. You only have to watch the latest celebrity, political, or sports fiasco to see this principle at work. One day people are regarded as heroes, and the next day they can't understand how it all went so bad so quickly.

Humility reverses the death spiral caused by arrogance. It's the first and most important step toward repairing our relationships with God and with the people around us. It might also be the hardest step, because our human nature is to try to rise above other people and not place ourselves below them. Our aspiration wants to climb the ladder, not hold the ladder for someone else. Our stubbornness wants to prove how right we are, and our selfishness cannot imagine putting someone else's needs ahead of our own.

And yet humility is the key to unlocking God's abundance in the workplace. Humility is a close cousin to a healthy others-first mentality, but it's an important attribute in its own right because it necessarily precedes thinking of others before we think of ourselves. If we humble ourselves before others, we will sincerely believe in our hearts that their needs come before our own. And if we humble ourselves before God, we will come to know that obedience to his wiser, stronger, more loving Spirit is simply a logical step.

If we truly believe that God has a better plan for us than we have for ourselves, then placing our lives in God's hands is no longer a leap of faith—it's simply a good decision. As a leader of my company, there isn't a more important step I can take than to turn the performance of the business over to the best leader our world has ever known. But I must first take the step of recognizing that God's abundance poured over my company is far greater than any results I could ever generate on my own.

Insanity: Believing That Our Children Might Actually Listen

I have attempted to pass the concept of humility on to both of my daughters. They are awesome women, but even in their twenties they have moments when they just can't seem to humble themselves with each other, with their friends, or with other people. This is true of many of us, but my daughters just happen to be the people I have observed most over the years.

While they were in high school and college, both of my daughters felt wronged if they got anything less than an A. One daughter—she's given me permission to tell on her—once received some pretty tough feedback about how she was perceived when it came to her participation in the classroom. In fact, she was told that she appeared to have an attitude, but what the professors didn't know (because she would not tell them) is that she is mostly deaf and cannot hear much of what is said. So to them it appeared that she was disinterested.

When her instructor gave her that feedback along with a low grade, it was like reality-TV drama in our house. "How dare she say such a thing? I care deeply about my classwork. I'm early to every class, and I complete every assignment. I sit up front, pay attention, and take notes. I got an A on every test and every paper except one. How can she say that I don't care?" This kind of lamentation went on for days.

I attempted to suggest that perhaps my daughter should listen to the feedback she received and try to learn from it. "Maybe," I said, "you could go in and explain your situation and apologize that you gave the wrong impression. Maybe you could ask for additional feedback about how to become a better student. I bet if you did that, she would have a completely different impression of you."

My suggestion went ignored for a week, but I'm pleased to report that the situation was resolved when my daughter decided that maybe she could indeed learn something from this experience. Just as Andrew's humility changed an entire business relationship in a single visit, my daughter's grade was improved when she humbled herself, accepted the feedback, and apologized to her professor. She had that same professor later on and got an A in the class.

A Biblical Case of Humility

There are many biblical stories about leaders achieving great success as a result of humility. We often find them in accounts of Old Testament battles waged in the face of overwhelming odds. David conquering Goliath is an obvious example, but many similar stores are found in the books of 1 and 2 Samuel and 1 and 2 Kings. In some of these stories, seemingly hopeless situations are resolved miraculously and at the last minute, when an enemy army crumbles before the battle even begins.

One great example is found in 2 Kings 18–19. Here we find the story of Sennacherib, the king of Assyria, who marched against Jerusalem with the mightiest army of its day. He sent messenger after messenger ahead of his army to Judah to tell King Hezekiah to surrender the city. Hezekiah knew that he was completely outmanned and that the people of Judah looked to him to solve this frightful problem.

But Hezekiah didn't even respond to the threat. He literally told his people not to answer Sennacherib's messengers. Each time he received a threatening demand, Hezekiah simply fell before God in humility and prayer. His people kept asking him what to do, and he kept telling them to trust in God. Thanks to this leader's humility, God destroyed the Assyrian army before they could ever attack the city.

A Biblical Case of Arrogance

Conversely, one of the most vivid examples of arrogance is found in Daniel 4. King Nebuchadnezzar considered himself the greatest king of

Babylon, the most powerful empire on earth. Daniel warned Nebuchadnezzar that God was going to deal with his pride if he didn't do it himself, but that didn't seem to make an impact. One evening, Nebuchadnezzar was standing on his roof surveying the city when he remarked to himself, "Is not this the great Babylon I have built as the royal residence, by my mighty power and for the glory of my majesty?" (Daniel 4:30).

In that moment, God took away the king's royal authority, and Nebuchadnezzar literally went insane. He became a madman. God sent him to live in the wild, eat grass like cattle, and be covered with the dew of heaven each morning. Nebuchadnezzar's hair grew long, and his nails became claw-like. For seven years he lived like a madman among the beasts of the field. At the end of those seven years, Nebuchadnezzar recorded this:

> At the end of that time, I, Nebuchadnezzar, raised my eyes toward heaven, and my sanity was restored. Then I praised the Most High; I honored and glorified him who lives forever. . . .
>
> At the same time that my sanity was restored, my honor and splendor were returned to me for the glory of my kingdom. My advisers and nobles sought me out, and I was restored to my throne and became even greater than before. Now I, Nebuchadnezzar, praise and exalt and glorify the King of heaven, because everything he does is right and all his ways are just. And those who walk in pride he is able to humble. (Daniel 4:34,36-37)

Can you imagine the nobles in Nebuchadnezzar's day saying to each other, "Gee, we need that crazy guy who's been living in the wild for the last seven years to come and lead us again — you know, the one who eats grass with claw hands and has wild hair. Anybody know that guy's cell number?"

Who in his right mind would do such a thing? No one, of course — unless God intervened to make the impossible happen. The Bible shows us that when we truly humble ourselves, God will restore our rightful place and make things even better than they were before. God can undo our mistakes and fix whatever mess we might get ourselves into.

How Big Is God?

If you've ever doubted just how big God is compared to our own human capabilities, I'd like you to think about the amazing universe he created. While we once thought that our planet was the center of the universe, we are now beginning to see just how vast and complex the universe actually is.

Most of us know that Earth and our solar system reside in the Milky Way galaxy. But what we might not completely understand is just how big our galaxy really is. To give you an idea of its size, consider that it would take you 100,000 years to travel from one end of the Milky Way galaxy to the other—that is, if you could travel the speed of light. If we assume an average human lifespan of 75 years, which is considered a generation, then we would learn that 1,333 generations would come and go before a light beam could travel the length of our galaxy.

Scientists estimate that there are seventy solar systems in our galaxy and that our sun is only one of 200 billion stars in the Milky Way alone. Just think of how massive and impressive our sun is, and then realize that there are 199,999,999,999 more of them in the Milky Way.

And that's only the beginning when it comes to the size of the universe. The closest galaxy to our own is Andromeda. It is 2.2 million light years away. A light year is about six trillion miles, so the Andromeda galaxy is 13.2 trillion miles away from the edge of the Milky Way, which we've already determined is 100,000 light years in length.

Still not enough to give you a sense of how much bigger God is than our individual human capability? While keeping in mind the size of the Milky Way and Andromeda galaxies, consider that recent estimates put the number of galaxies in the known universe at 500 billion!

And who knows, really, how much bigger the universe actually is? That's all we can tell for now with our current technology. Are there more galaxies that we're not aware of? More universes?

Learning these facts made me drop to my knees. I am in awe of what God created when he spoke the earth and stars into being. When I think about how much of it I don't understand, I am humbled beyond words at the majesty of his creation. My problems, my selfish desires, my petty grievances, and my drama all just melt away. How can I even begin to think that I could know better than such a powerful, amazing force? I am in awe. I am left speechless. I shut my mouth.

C. S. Lewis put it this way: "In God you come up against something which is in every respect immeasurably superior to yourself. Unless you know God as that — and, therefore, know yourself as nothing in comparison — you do not know God at all. As long as you are proud you cannot know God."

Humility Is Top Priority

Knowing God is, of course, a prerequisite to putting him to work. And humility is a prerequisite to knowing God. It is our all-important first step. When my good friend Dave first started working with me to help deepen my faith walk, humility was part of every conversation. After every meeting, Dave would say gently but firmly, "Stay humble, Scott."

By this point in my life, I honestly thought I had become at least somewhat humble. But until Dave said it to me about fifty times, I didn't realize how not-so-humble I could be. Arrogance and pride can be very subtle residents within a person's heart, even within a Christian's heart. We think we have risen above conceit until we really start examining our thoughts, actions, and motivations. Even a prideful *thought* can come across in our actions without us even realizing it. We think that we've moved past it, but those around us know better. What's more important, God knows better.

The Bible teaches that unless we are attached to the Vine (Jesus), we are nothing. It doesn't say that we are okay. It doesn't say that we can work really hard to do our best. It says that we are *nothing* without him. Until we humble ourselves to recognize that we need to abide in Christ, we will *have* nothing and we will *offer* nothing to anyone else. We will simply spin and toil away in our own strength. It might feel like we are making progress, but it will be work built upon sand. A humble focus on God will make our foundation as solid as a rock.

Snake Oil Salesmen Are People Too

I'll share one final example of how humility can change the face of business. In the 1980s my friend John had a vision for two companies to merge and focus on a particular market segment. We'll simply call them Company A and Company B. John began the work of convincing the two companies to join forces. While it took a couple of years to make it happen, the two organizations finally announced a joint venture.

In principle, the idea was brilliant. In practice, it was a very tough road. Company A and Company B had very different cultures and extremely different views on how to run a business. There was also significant disagreement within each company about whether the joint venture was a good move. John not only had to convince both companies to work together across company lines, but he also had to help managers within each company reach consensus that this idea had any hope for success. It was a chaotic mix of ideas, disciplines, and skill sets.

I worked for Company B at the time of the joint venture and was one of the first joint-venture employees. Those of us on the front lines were putting in eighty-hour work weeks—only to get berated by both Company A managers and Company B managers. Making one side happy enraged the other side. I can remember on more than one occasion being outraged at some of the commentary and barely containing an intense desire to lash back at the barbs coming my way.

But John was persistent and took it all in stride. He would come to the meetings and take all the flack without emotion. Although he was a high-level leader in the organization, he would sit there as managers several levels below him called him anything from a snake oil salesman to a liar. John never reacted to the provocations. He calmly took notes and responded with logic and encouragement about why we needed to stick with it. "Our customers," he would say, "will respond to what we are doing. We just need time for the rest of the market to catch up."

Hardly anyone believed it, but a few of us kept working away, and after a couple of years we began to see signs of a turn. Before long, the business had doubled. Then it doubled again. When Company A and Company B first joined forces, the combined business had been worth $200 million. Within seven years the business was driving more than $1 billion per year in revenue. Within fifteen years it was more than $2 billion.

Today, almost twenty-five years later, the division that was created from this joint venture is the largest and most valued segment of the company that bought the business. They still have a dominant lock on their market, and their competitors have struggled to make even a dent in their leadership spot.

None of this would have happened without John's humility. For years, people with less vision, intelligence, and stature had denigrated this brilliant, accomplished, and passionate man. On more than one occasion, John was verbally abused and almost fired over his idea. Had I been in his place, I would have quit many years earlier. No one deserves that kind of abuse. But John never complained. He simply persisted, confident that the path he was on would be successful someday. It was just a matter of time.

A humble spirit caused John to be *patient*. It enabled him to listen to what people needed so that he could adapt his vision to suit the many constituents he needed for the joint venture to succeed. Humility also gave John the strength to be *persistent*. It created in him the flexibility necessary to allow the vision to grow at a pace that the organization could absorb rather than at the faster pace he was far more capable of maintaining. John set the example of what humility can do when matched with strong vision, determination, and hard work.

I can promise you that without John this business would have failed and would not look anything like it does today. Instead, it is a massive enterprise and the crown jewel of a much larger organization. The humility of just one man changed an entire industry. Just imagine what could follow if entire cultures became humble and obedient: Even greater things than this could be accomplished.

As you think about your daily workload and any big vision you might have, what is your theology? Would you rather seek to do it on your own or have God do it through you? It's a simple question, but it's the difference between a life of struggle and a life of abundance. Are you a Bailey, or are you a Max? I love them both, but one gets more of my attention than the other only because he asks for it.

For Reflection and Discussion

1. In what ways is your theology like a cat's or a dog's relationship with its owner?
2. How would you define humility? What does it mean to be humble? What is the opposite of humility?
3. Is humility the most important step in a relationship with God, or are there any other traits that are more important?
4. What does it mean that if we are not attached to the Vine, we are "nothing"? Don't non-Christians feel like "something"?
5. Are we here to serve God, or is he here to serve us? (The answer to this question should be obvious, but now look at your behavior and respond to the question honestly from the standpoint of how you tend to think and act.)
6. As an accomplished leader, how would you respond if someone below your rank called you a snake oil salesman? Could you handle it the same way John did and build a business worth $2 billion in the process?
7. As a leader faced with overwhelming odds, could you have come before God with humility the way Hezekiah did? He was the king of Judah, and yet he told his subjects that only God had the answer to the massive threat. Can you imagine what his people

were thinking when he kept going to his chambers in prayer? So many of his subjects must have been saying, "Do something! Stop praying and do something! The enemy is at the gate. Take the lead! Aren't you king?" Would you be willing to let people think less of you as the leader of a nation even though you were spending your time in the right place?

Preparation for the Week Ahead

During the next week on the job, try to be aware of when you are acting out of arrogance (either overtly or subtly) and when you are acting out of humility. What kind of response do you get in either situation? Which attitude truly makes you feel better inside?

A Prayer for the Week Ahead

Father, I know that selfish desires usually drive my behavior. I ask that you intervene this week and undo my natural instinct for self-preservation and self-pleasure. Cause me to have a servant's heart. Instill in me the desire to lift up others. Help me ask only to be a blessing to other people rather than ask you to heap blessings upon me. Help tame my arrogance, my pride, and my willful behavior. Help me to want success for others more than I want it for myself. Help me to make it my primary goal to advance your kingdom rather than to advance my own personal agenda. I ask all of this in Christ's holy name. Amen.

Don't Be a Patsy
(but Don't Be a Jerk Either)

So he made a whip out of cords, and drove all from the temple area... he scattered the coins of the money changers and overturned their tables. To those who sold doves he said, "Get these out of here! How dare you turn my Father's house into a market!"

—JOHN 2:15-16

I feel the need to rescue some readers who might be struggling after the first few chapters. If you're anything like I was not so long ago, you're reading this stuff only because someone told you that you should read it. Or you're reading it because you intellectually get that this stuff is probably right, but nevertheless it still feels like a load of soft, lovey-dovey hoo-haa.

You might be among those who have built their entire working persona upon a tough, street-smart approach to their jobs. To you, this whole "humility and others-first thing" might sound wimpy and ineffectual, especially if you're in a position of authority. If you consider yourself to be a leader of people in any realm, you might be grappling with how to apply these be-nice concepts to a harsh working world.

A leader is supposed to be strong, take risks, provide direction, and make the tough calls. A leader sometimes has to manage through conflict and hire, fire, and discipline people. He or she sometimes has to disagree with, push, and challenge both people and organizations. And many Christian leaders work in a secular world in which some people might try to take advantage of them.

Sometimes a leader has to be the sole voice of dissent in a room filled with yes-people. He or she often sees things differently from the rest of the organization and needs to challenge the thinking of other very talented people, some of whom might have big egos and aggression to match. Leadership by its very nature means standing out from the crowd.

You might wonder how all of this squares with humility and service to others. After all, if you were to show up at work as a soft, timid, no-opinion flip-flopper, then you'd offer no value to your team and no usefulness to your organization. Anyone who seeks complete harmony, meaning no disagreement, pushback, or debate, simply propagates the status quo, which ultimately leads to the decline of any enterprise. These no-conflict types might be very nice people to whom you'd want to live next door, but you don't want them working with you or for you because they are completely ineffective.

Let me state unequivocally that I am not recommending that anyone go wimpy. The greatest servant-leader the world has ever known was a stir-the-pot kind of guy. In the passage at the start of this chapter, Jesus fashioned a whip and drove both people and animals out of the temple. He turned over the tables of the money changers and told them to "get out of here." This was an extremely unpopular move, but it was the right move. He stood firm, and he stood alone. Nothing wimpy about him!

In Matthew 23, Jesus lambasted the scribes and Pharisees — the religious elite of his day — as evil hypocrites. In Matthew 24–25, he repeatedly asserted that unless we are attentive to his presence, he will not "know us" when the time comes to enter into the kingdom of heaven. This kind of commentary occurs frequently throughout the New Testament.

The life of Christ doesn't exactly paint a picture of a peace-at-all-costs, don't-rock-the-boat, don't-risk-offending-anyone, let's-hold-hands-and-sing-kumbaya kind of guy. Jesus was tough when he needed to be. He got angry, frustrated, dismissive, and downright aggressive with people who did not have a true heart. You either got it or you didn't. And if you didn't, he would quickly move on to someone who was more open and obedient to the Word. He was strong, clear, and not at all afraid to get in your face if you were self-absorbed, hypocritical, or otherwise misrepresenting the way of God.

He was firm, and he was fair.

The Humble Messiah

But there's an important difference between Jesus and the rest of us (besides him being the Messiah, of course). The Bible tells us that Jesus voluntarily set aside his divine rights and attributes, humbling himself to become a man. Thus, during his thirty-three years on earth, in everything that he did he relied on the indwelling power of the Holy Spirit and on God's Word. Jesus spent much time alone with God in prayer. He never did anything for personal gain—all of his teachings and actions were to advance the kingdom. That was his only agenda. He didn't care what people thought of him. He cared only about what would glorify God.

So whenever Jesus opened his mouth, took a step, healed someone, or miraculously fed thousands, he had already humbled himself before his heavenly Father, acknowledging his dependence on God's help. This left him *empty of himself but filled with God's wisdom, power, and direction*. With that confidence, Christ had no time for human nature or the games that people play. He was not here to please men and women but to please God. He was not here to appease human frailties; he was here to help humanity see the new path to the kingdom (see John 14:6).

Because Jesus was acting in their best interests, he was not afraid to push people to their greatest potential. He was strong enough and direct enough to rouse them from their spiritual slumber. Though he was history's all-time greatest servant-leader, humility did not call for Christ to be subservient to the world. He rejected the world's ways, sometimes aggressively. Humility did not ask him to bow down to meet the selfish needs of a people who were more concerned about what they lacked than for what they could have in him. Jesus simply obeyed God and would not let anything stand in the way of that path.

The lesson we can learn from this is that humility and service are not the same as subservience. Humility simply directs us to listen before speaking and to pray before acting. *It requires us to be in community with others only after being in communion with God.* Once we have listened to and submitted to God's Word, we are then called to be dedicated and passionate about the path he has shown us. We can proceed with all the confidence that accompanies knowing that we are following the Creator's will and guidance. *Although it might sound contradictory, there is no one stronger and more self-assured than the humble man or woman whose confidence is placed in the God of the universe.*

I can assure you that no one would ever accuse me of being soft in the workplace. In fact, I'm often accused of being a contrarian — even downright stubborn. I don't particularly like being regarded in those terms, but these perceptions are probably fair — in part because I'm still growing in my faith and my human nature is more out in front than I'd like it to be. But I think that another reason for why I'm perceived in this way is that I spend regular time with God in prayer and, therefore, I'm confident in the path he has outlined for me.

As long as I have sought out and listened to God and the people I serve, then I will be stubborn and obedient to the path that has been made clear. I'm not fearful or concerned about getting fired or upsetting or pleasing people. All those things might happen, but they'd be secondary to God's greater plan. My primary goal is always to serve, inspire, encourage, and promote a culture of love. But I will also stand firm if a situation falls out of line with God's Word. This, I believe, is true humility, the kind modeled by Jesus himself and what I try to live out every day.

Good People, Bad Intent

I've been called upon to be firm on more than one occasion in my career, usually when turning around troubled businesses. Turnaround environments often involve great pain in dealing with employees, unions, vendors, and customers — none of whom are happy when I walk through the door. By the time I step in, the business is sometimes badly broken. People are in distress from the start, and when people are upset it can bring out the worst in them.

In one turnaround situation, the company was losing $3 million monthly before I arrived. People were quitting every day, and the supplier community had put them on credit hold. The former owners had used some very creative accounting, and by the time it was discovered by an audit team, the balance sheet was in such a mess that it took us two years to uncover all the surprises. The previous owners also had started paying people cash bonuses to keep them working. It became nearly impossible to get anyone back to work under normal business conditions.

Our team began the work of overlaying a set of values and disciplines upon a broken, corrupt workplace. Some of the people were very grateful to be operating justly again, but many others started to revolt. Our competitors hired many of these angry people away from us and, in turn, stole our customers — some of whom also had become accustomed to the under-the-table environment.

But that was only part of the challenge. Our business operated twenty-four hours a day, and it was not uncommon for me to enter the warehouse at 2 a.m. to find some of the former employees in our building, handing out job applications to my people. They were holding competitive recruiting fairs right in our own building! It turned out that some of the associates who stayed with us were helping their former friends steal not only our people and our customers but also our products right off the warehouse shelves.

Perhaps worst of all, it seemed that our competitors knew every move we were making or were about to make. Every time we set up a new way to do something, our competitors beat us to the punch. Every time we bid on a new piece of business, our competitors seemed to know the price we would propose. They also seemed to know our most profitable routes, and they poached our sales people, drivers, and pickers assigned to those operations. I wondered if perhaps our office was bugged, so we had some techno-experts come in to do a sweep, but nothing nefarious was found. Still, there was something wrong going on, and we just couldn't nail it down.

What we later uncovered was that a few members of the team that I inherited had been funneling some of our confidential information to their former coworkers who had left the company. Uncertain whether our business would survive, they were giving themselves an escape hatch by ingratiating themselves to the competition just in case they needed a job. They weren't taking money; they were just trying to position themselves for future employment if that became necessary.

What you might be surprised to hear me say is that these were not bad people. They were good family men and women who were, for the most part, decent human beings. But I can't think of a better example of how not to act at work. By putting themselves first, they resorted to underhanded behavior that jeopardized an entire company and the five hundred people who worked there. They caused great pain for many people who spent countless hours away from their family trying to undo all the damage that had been done.

These self-first people created stress, bad feelings, and in some cases despair among other employees whose jobs had to be eliminated as our customers melted away. For more than one person, the resulting daily tensions brought on health problems. All of this damage and jeopardy happened because a few people decided to act unfaithfully in order to secure a job elsewhere if things got worse at our company. While I understood their desire to protect themselves, their actions were completely unacceptable. We could not tolerate such behavior.

One night I stayed very late. The front office was empty. In my office, I dropped to my knees and turned the business over to God. I knew that I could not fix it on my own. I needed guidance, I needed support, and I needed a miracle. There were too many problems and too much corruption — not just business corruption but corruption of the spirit. Only God could undo the web of deceit and the severe damage it had wrought.

Step by step, we gradually identified, addressed, and dismantled the problems these disloyal people had caused. After they departed our company, we continued investigating and slowly removed anyone else who had aligned with their cancerous, negative attitude. While this created more short-term pain, it began cleansing the poison from the work environment and assured our faithful employees that we were committed to building a culture of integrity and others-first humility. We carefully screened new hires to ensure that they would bring honesty, loyalty, and energy to the job. Slowly the business began to turn around as a new culture began to grow within the company.

Within eighteen months, we were making more than $1 million a month and had cleaned up more than $20 million of the problems on the balance sheet. In just two years, the business had swung $50 million annually to the positive in bottom-line performance. The balance sheet fraud had been written off and completely cleaned up.

Obviously, it wasn't me who created that turnaround. It was the work of hundreds of dedicated people and the blessings of a God who responded when people brought humility and a sense of service to the job. It would take a few more years for the complete turnaround to take hold, but the process began during some of those darkest moments when good people stood up for what they believed.

God's Agenda or Yours?

You can be tough when dealing with the world — but only if you don't have an agenda that involves your own personal gain in status, compensation, or self-aggrandizement. You can also be tough with people who have either lost their way or are not living up to their potential. If they have grown too comfortable in their surroundings or arrogant about their performance, then you might need to make them a bit uncomfortable in order to help them rediscover humility and stay sharp.

You might think that the funny title of this chapter, "Don't Be a Patsy," sounds a bit odd for a book about bringing God into your workplace. But the point I hope to make is that being obedient to God does not mean becoming a shrinking violet. There are times when God uses forcefulness if other means are not effective. He also uses strong people to accomplish his direction and to lead other people to a better path. Just read 1 and 2 Samuel to learn how forceful David was in his lifetime. This man of God was repeatedly called upon to be a very tough-minded leader. He was fair but firm.

But while I hope to make the point that we need not go soft to be Christlike and humble, I could have spent a lot more time on the "Don't Be a Jerk" part of this chapter. Just because we're on God's path doesn't mean that it's okay to become self-righteous. Despite our best intentions, we're still human, and we'll still fail. Sometimes it is far too easy to let confidence become cockiness. It's too easy to become arrogant or self-righteous about being on the right path. And if we do become arrogant or self-righteous, we'll fall off the path just as quickly as those whom God has sent us to serve.

We need to hold humility, compassion, and understanding in our hearts even while we are doing the tough work that needs to be done. When doing the difficult job at hand, honor the people around you — even your so-called enemies. Jesus told us to love our enemies and to pray for those who mistreat us (see Matthew 5:44). That's not only counterintuitive, but it's also countercultural — and extremely difficult to do. It takes true humility, the kind that emanates from God's Spirit within us. The way we act with our enemies might be the very thing that turns them to Christ or away from Christ.

God does not take joy in overcoming hypocrisy or worldly issues. He knows that he has already won, so there's nothing to be joyful about when dealing with the tough stuff of our society. He simply does what has to be done. He calls us to be loving and compassionate but also to stand firm in the face of injustice. Stay in constant contact with the Holy Spirit, and follow the guidance you receive minute by minute. Humble confidence will keep you strong when strength is the response God wants.

For Reflection and Discussion

1. Why do you think Jesus was so hard on the Pharisees?
2. In Matthew 15:27, Jesus uses an analogy of a dog when denying a woman the help she is asking for. That's not exactly a loving way to say no. Why do you think he was so dismissive of this woman?
3. Is it possible to be firm, loving, and tough all at once? Can you think of an example?
4. The book of Proverbs tells us that when we spare the rod, we spoil the child. In what ways might this be true with adults as well?
5. In what ways is God tough with us at times? Think of an example or two and the lesson you learned (or should have learned) from the experience.
6. In the past few years, in what situations were you called upon to be firm? How well did you respond to that challenge? Were you fair? Firm? Brutal? Did you respond from your own ego, or was firmness the godly response?
7. How can you create a culture of love and discipline at the same time?

Preparation for the Week Ahead

Think about areas in your life in which perhaps you are being too soft. Are you serving God in that situation, or are you avoiding conflict simply to please other people and make it easier on yourself?

When you noticed that you were firm, were you arrogant in that firmness—perhaps a bit self-righteous in the process? Or was it a gentle firmness based on love and another person's best interests?

When you feel strongly about something, is it to promote your agenda or God's agenda?

A Prayer for the Week Ahead

Father, I seek your guidance to know when to back off and when to press forward. I ask for the ability to discern between my own agenda and your agenda before I react strongly to the people and events I'll encounter in the week ahead. Show me how to live in Christlike, humble strength this week. Help me to be forceful when I need to be forceful and gentle when I need to be gentle. I pray this in the name of your Son Jesus. Amen.

5

Blame It on Bush

PRINCIPLE 5: *Access divine power.*

I tell you the truth, anyone who has faith in me will do what I have been doing. He will do even greater things than these, because I am going to the Father.

—JOHN 14:12

Recently I had the opportunity to have dinner with George W. and Laura Bush at their Dallas home to support a charity that was honoring former Dallas Cowboys running back and NFL Hall of Famer Emmitt Smith. It was one of the coolest things I've ever done. Regardless of what you think about his politics, to have dinner at the home of a former president of the United States is really something special.

When I received the invitation, I thought someone was playing a joke on me. Some due diligence finally convinced me that the invitation was real, so I made plans to fly to Texas. All along, I assumed that while the Bushes had made their home available, they would not be there in person; or if they did come, they'd waltz in for five minutes, wave at everyone, and then leave.

I arrived at the airport and made my way to the dinner. As I approached their neighborhood, I was still skeptical of what might happen. The valet took my car, and I walked toward the front door. Again, I expected nothing extraordinary—I just assumed that I'd mingle with the thirty or so guests who were just like me, normal people doing normal things.

I wasn't even certain if I was in the right place. The home was very nice but modest. There was not a crowd. And there was no visible security, although I'm sure it was there. If it had not been for the valet parking, I would have thought that someone would come to the door and say, "Oh no, you have the wrong place. They live in the palace down the street."

But when we got to the front door, the person greeting us was President George W. Bush himself. Now, I need to take a brief detour for a moment; there's something you need to know about me that is relevant to this story. I used to be a celebrity bodyguard. One of the reasons I was so effective in that job was that I don't get starstruck. I will treat a celebrity with respect, but I treat everyone else with the same respect. Famous people don't amaze me any more than I'm amazed by the miracle of you and me. I just don't go gaga (pun intended) over the latest movie star or musician.

But there I was, at the front door of George W. Bush's house, being greeted by George W. Bush himself—and I basically froze. I'm typically pretty good on my feet, but that was not the case this time. About the best I could muster was, "How are you, Mr. President?" He answered enthusiastically, "I'm doing great. Just great." I thanked him for having me over to his home and then proceeded to chat with his wife, Laura, who was standing right next to him.

The Bushes are some of the most gracious hosts you'd ever want to meet. They stayed the entire time and visited with everyone. They spoke beautifully about the cause we were there to support and about the honoree, Emmitt Smith. I might add that the Smith family is also amazing, gracious, and humble. I was blown away by the whole thing. I was indeed starstruck.

It got me thinking about why I was so blown away. I think it's because I'm a big football fan and, when it comes to my country, I'm a syrupy guy. I love the United States, and I'm over-the-top proud of it. I sometimes get weepy when the national anthem is played, in particular at events honoring soldiers or people who have sacrificed to serve our country. So to have chitchatted with a former president of the United States right in the comfort of his own home was more than my patriotic fervor could stand.

But as excited as I still am about this, I realize that I had been getting very wrapped up in the worldly nature of it all. I had dinner with the leader of the most powerful nation on the planet, and I was really excited about that. Would I have gotten just as excited about meeting a woman who takes in foster children and provides them with a life they never would have had otherwise? Would I have been as excited to meet Christians in distant nations who are willing to die for their faith?

Worldly power and celebrity, as cool and as important as they are to us, are not what God wants us to focus on. (I'd be willing to bet that both George W. and Laura Bush would agree with that.) In fact, the Bible tells us again and again that we are to reject worldly power or status and turn our eyes to what cannot be seen. We are to worship God, not the things of this world. And for those of us who have positions of power, we are to constantly pray to bring God into our leadership role so that we operate from a holy perspective instead of a worldly perspective. But worshiping something unseen is not a natural thing for humans to do, and most people don't even care to do so in the first place.

Catching Flies

If you look up the word *power* on wikipedia.com, you'll find the following definition: "Power refers broadly to any ability to effect change or exert control over either things or people, subjects or objects." Isn't that just how the world views power—as exerting control over things or people? The world views power as a grand manipulation, a game of sorts, aimed at taking authority and using it to its advantage rather than to the advantage of some higher purpose.

The natural human response is to want power and influence over our lives and over others who are in our lives. We want stuff, and we will do almost anything to get the things we want! Sometimes that desire appears as passive-aggressive manipulation, and sometimes it's in-your-face conflict or even violence. But most of the time it's a much more subtle form of exploitation: If we can get the things we need by being nice, then we'll be nice. The axiom "You can catch more flies with honey than with vinegar" is born from that mentality.

But even when we use honey, for most of us the primary goal is to get. In other words, we're still trying to catch flies; it's just the way we go about it that separates one person from another. Sometimes those "flies" are materialistic items like cars, toys, and electronics. Sometimes they are more security-related like shelter, food, clothing, and hearty investment balances. Other times, we might seek a more emotional payoff, such as status, prestige, love, friendship, or a sense of belonging.

But when we finally do get what we want, we're never completely satisfied for long, are we? No matter how much we have, we always want more. *Our focus rarely stays on what we have but instead on what we don't have.* We figure that in order to get more we really need to have more power. More power and more stuff for me mean less for you.

Most people don't even recognize that they think or act this way because they believe themselves to be good. And they probably are good most of the time. Indeed, the pull of power and the stuff we think it can provide is a very subtle urge within all of us. But it's there, and it always wants *more*. It grows slowly over time — so slowly that we usually don't even recognize its seductive tug.

Sometimes our drive for power is held back for years until it is suddenly unleashed in a strong show of force, not unlike a surprise military barrage. But more often than not the quest for power is a gradual, unspoken bartering process. I'll sign this treaty but only if we get access to your economy. I'll show you love if you show me love. I'll give you friendship if you're there for me when times are tough. I'll serve my employers but only if they pay me what I think I'm worth. I'll stay in this job for now, but I'm gone the first time someone offers me more money or a better title. I'll stay with that new company only as long as it serves my needs, and then I'll move on to the greener pasture.

We use people, corporations, and governments as stepping stones to the "next big thing" that will bring us more of what we think we need—money, things, security, or love. It's human nature. While some of us have more control over that part of our lives than others, it's innately built into our survival instinct. It's why the Bible so often refers to the importance of transcending self, because the self is overly concerned about things of this world and because it can act so selfishly without our even being aware that it's happening.

Great People, Great Faith, Great Power

Regardless of whether it's intentional, we are conditioned by society to believe that personal power is a necessary component of success. Yet the most powerful man who ever lived did absolutely nothing for himself. The leader who has changed the lives of hundreds of millions of people lived not as the king that he truly is but as a servant-leader. He was born into poverty with nothing but a lineage and a promise. He never asked for anything, but he gave everything. He was humiliated, beaten, and killed for his cause. And just before his death, he was a servant-leader to the very man who had betrayed him unto death—when he could have ruled over the miscreant with a vengeance.

Yet it is Jesus whom people look to for strength, assurance, and trust two thousand years after his ascension. It is not the powerful ruler of his day whom we follow but the humble servant who changed the world and earned our devotion and praise forever. It is the man who gave away his power to others who changed the world then and now and set the example for us to follow.

Many others throughout history have done something similar. They gave away their authority and status and in the process ended up with more personal power than the greatest political leaders of their day—power that lives on even after their deaths. Because they accessed divine power, they transcended anything they might have done on their own.

- Gandhi was an English-trained lawyer before he gave up his profession to dedicate his life to the people of his country. He has inspired millions to a life of service and is loved and respected by people of all faiths.
- Martin Luther King Jr. not only preached peace and service to others, but he also lived his life as an example of what it means to put others ahead of self.
- Mother Teresa dedicated her entire life to serving others ahead of self and is now considered a saint.
- Moses had a life of luxury, living in Pharaoh's good graces until he gave it all up to serve his people. His life still inspires millions of Jews and Christians as a key foundation-builder of their faith.

Each of these leaders demonstrated two things in common: humility and service. None had aspirations for fame or success. In fact, most gave up the success they had already achieved in order to live more humble lives, yet they became some of the most powerful, effective people the world has ever known. They set out to serve their God and to help humanity, but in the process they gained more power and influence than those who have gone after power, fame, and fortune in the first place.

These leaders did not rule over anyone. They inspired. They spoke not just to the mind but mainly to the spirit. They called forth the best in the people who followed them and in the process unleashed all their passion, creativity, and energy. *When people engage with their spirit, you get all the benefits of their intellectual skill, but you also get the benefit of the fire in their belly—and that is where battles are won or lost.*

We've all heard legendary stories about Ritz Carlton hotels and Nordstrom department stores, where employees are given authority to make on-the-spot decisions when extraordinary customer service is called for. Many years after the stories actually take place, these companies are still known for their loyal customers who are willing to pay more to patronize them because the service experience is so exceptional.

One of the founders of the Ritz Carlton brand is Horst Schulze. Horst is known for his dedication to company associates and for the way he makes sure that each associate is acutely aware of the greater purpose of the organization. He personally visits with new associates to ensure that they know they are empowered to achieve the lofty goals of the organization.

Horst also has strong views on what it means to lead an organization. The lowest form of leadership, in his opinion, is management—people who simply direct workers in the doing of their jobs. The highest form of leadership, in Horst's view, is when leaders inspire associates to perform beyond the technical aspects of their jobs and serve in a way perhaps never before imagined. It is in this way that organizations become known as exceptional brands as well as preferred employers for the most talented people in any industry.

Capturing Hearts, Minds, and Spirits

In one large-scale business in which I worked alongside an awesome team of high-performing leaders, we decided that one of our strategies would be to become the preferred employer in our business. We set a course to head down that path but realized that we needed to measure where we stood at the moment. We hired an outside firm to measure employee engagement among the people in our business. Engagement is *not* satisfaction; satisfaction is simply the next level up from feeling nothing at all. Engagement, on the other hand, measures the number of people who truly get what you do and are deeply loyal to your cause.

We were distressed to learn that only 42 percent of our associates were engaged with us and our mission. We talked with our managers about the need to do much better in this area, but the next year our level of engagement registered only 45 percent. This told us that we had not even engaged our managers in the business let alone the twenty thousand frontline associates who were closest to our customers.

We spent the bulk of the following year focused on little else but how to better engage our people. We emphasized people management first and foremost in our culture, and we backed this up with training and tools to help our managers do better jobs of leading and not just managing our people. That year our engagement level jumped to 69 percent, which we were told was the best practice in our industry. As the journey progressed and our engagement scores continued to improve, so did our bottom line.

When we first started surveying our people, we used a relatively small 10-percent sample of our company and received a not-atypical 25-percent response. Within five years, we surveyed 100 percent of our associates and got a 92-percent response. People became more assured that if they offered feedback, the company would do something about it and the culture would change for the better.

When we put our people first, our profits soared. More than that, our people had more fun in the business. Our turnover rate dropped to a third of its former level, and our business grew faster, allowing more opportunity for everyone in the company. We were later named one of the best 125 training companies in the world and one of the best 100 Web-based training companies in the world. All of this started when some leaders decided that serving our associates mattered as much or more than the numbers we were producing at the time. It grew into something great as we learned to speak to the heart and not just the minds of our people.

Leadership at Home

We can also see this leadership dynamic play out in our community and our home. For those of us with children, we experience the drama that accompanies trying to manage (rather than lead) our little ones. While very young, children need to be told what to do because they literally cannot fend for themselves. There comes a time, however, when they grow to resent that direction, and they rebel. The battle that ensues during the teenage years becomes a test of wills that can wreak havoc for both the parents and the child. Arguments, trouble, and pain result when each side of the equation tries to demonstrate who has the power in the relationship.

The trick is to find ways to engage your children the same way that you would engage your associates at work. They need to see something that *attracts* them rather than forces them into any particular area. While I figured this out way too late as a dad, I finally came to see that my job was to inspire more than direct my children. My job was to daily access God's power and guidance so that my behavior and attitude would better reflect Christ to them as an example to follow. If I followed the principle of abiding in Christ's peace and power, then perhaps it would be a model they would want to follow in their lives. (I failed miserably at this for a very long time!)

If they ever wanted advice, I would simply offer what was working for me and encourage them to discover if it worked for them. Even now, during their young adulthood, I am still tempted to be like a dad and tell them how to do this or that, and I'm sure they think I fall back into that mode more often than they'd like. But I hope I've done a better job of serving them in a way that reflects Christ's love more than the way I'd like things to be done. When I'm abiding in Christ and yielding to his divine power, I'm far better at engaging rather than instructing — to lead as I would want to be led.

He's a King, not Santa Claus

There is power in a life of service that exceeds any power imposed upon you by title, regardless of whether your role is prince, parent, president, or police officer. It is that power you will tap into that will make you more effective in all your relationships, including those at work and at home. *It's not a power that is bestowed upon you. It's a power that works through you to produce results. It's a power that is unleashed only after you have surrendered any thoughts of personal gain.*

The power we can access from God is not like becoming Santa Claus. It's not a power intended to make you more popular or successful. It's a power that is unleashed when you want that power to work for somebody or something other than you. The irony is that as soon as you want power more for other people than yourself, *you actually become more powerful.*

I encourage you to read chapters 14–17 of the gospel of John. In chapters 14–16, John very clearly tells us how to access divine power. As we abide in Jesus Christ and follow his commands, God's Holy Spirit literally resides within our being. It is as we abide in Christ that we have access to the divine power of God.

If you've ever wondered why your prayers might not be answered, these three chapters tell you why. If we are not following Christ's commands, then we are living in sin, and unconfessed sin disrupts our fellowship with him and our access to his power. A big part of abiding in Christ is keeping short accounts with God by living the promise of 1 John 1:9: "If we confess our sins, he is faithful and just and will forgive us our sins and purify us from all unrighteousness." Confessing our sins and appropriating God's forgiveness restores fellowship with him through the Holy Spirit, reinvigorating the abiding relationship. It is only as we *abide in him, align with his will, and then ask in his name* that our prayers are answered.

In John 17, we see how Christ prays for his people—his *team,* so to speak. He prays for their protection and for their souls. He prays for their strength and for wisdom. He prays for them to access the power of God so they will be able to do even greater things than he did while on earth. What if we, as leaders, managers, and parents were to pray in the same way for the people under our care?

Shifting Prayers from Internal to External

As I studied these chapters in John, I slowly realized (painfully) that my personal prayer life had almost always been entirely centered on me—on what I needed, what I wanted, and how I wanted my prayers to be answered. But all of what Christ prayed for was to glorify God, even if that meant praying for his enemies, the very people who wanted to kill him. Because his motive was to serve God and others rather than himself, God answered every one of his prayers.

If we start viewing our circumstances as an opportunity to glorify God, then the bad stuff seems more like an opportunity than a problem. The worse the problem, the greater the opportunity! And if our prayer life shifts to how we can better serve the people around us, then our goals align with God's goals. And once we are in alignment with God, there is no limit to what we can accomplish.

The irony of this entire book is that in order for you to put God to work, *you're going to have to stop caring so much about what God does* for *you and care more about what he does* through *you*. When you release the natural, very human, selfish desire for power and success and things, God's abundance will pour out upon you and everyone and everything you touch.

If you are a failure at work, what nonbelievers will want to follow you? They'll see your sacrificial-lamb act as something to be ridiculed rather than admired. On the other hand, if they see a godly person being successful, they'll be more likely to pay attention and listen to what you have to say. Your success becomes your platform to change lives, and God will continue to make that platform stronger when he sees you use it for his glory. But if you turn that success into a shrine of your own achievements, then God will no longer have any use for your wealth and stature.

This hit home with me recently as I put my bio and résumé together to help my wife get started in her own business. Now that our children are grown, she was looking to start a franchise store, and I was being asked to sign a personal guarantee. There were several requests for my business experience: from the bank providing the loan, the landlord providing the space, and the franchisor who wanted to know if they were getting into business with reasonable people.

Along the way, about ten different people read my résumé and told my wife how impressive it was. Loans were approved immediately, and everything else fell right into place. At first I was shocked. I knew that I had attained some measure of success, but I'm usually one to focus on the things I have *not* succeeded at rather than the things that have worked out. It caught me off guard that so many people thought so much of my career.

That shock gradually morphed into mild appreciation for their kind words and then into outright pride that my accomplishments were so admired. But at that point, not-so-amazingly, everything started going wrong. The franchise agreement soured, and the lease contracts got bogged down in committee. The loan became very complicated, and the whole thing started going south. I got rather indignant that people would dare question me, what with all of my business savvy. I started viewing the people in the process as enemies in the way of my success and idiots who didn't know what they were doing.

I was no longer glorifying God. I had taken the platform he had built for me and enshrined it with trophies glorifying *me*. I embarrassed myself with the people we were doing business with and was the opposite of a good example. With that, God pulled the rug out from under me and sent me facedown, begging for forgiveness that I was exalting myself and not my heavenly Father.

Our prayers are answered when we obey and are in alignment with God's will. Our prayers are answered when we align our thoughts with his thoughts. Our goals are in alignment with God when we seek to advance his kingdom. And his divine power flows through us when we allow him to take control.

For Reflection and Discussion

1. How can it be that in order to get results you have to stop asking for results?
2. Is it wrong to pray for results?
3. What good is divine power if in order to get it you have to give up thoughts of personal gain?
4. Is God or should God be a wish-granter?
5. How do you give God room to move in your life?
6. What does it look like to give God room to move in your life?

7. What would it mean to you if you had the power of the Creator at your disposal? What would you do with it if you had it? What if you already have it and you just don't know it?

8. If you give frontline associates the power to make individual decisions, does that unleash creativity or chaos? What would it take to give it a try?

9. Have you ever met a celebrity or a public figure whom you very much respect? How did you feel? Did you get nervous or anxious? If so, why do you think that it made you feel different from meeting any "normal" person on the street?

10. Why is our culture so fixated on celebrity?

11. Is it possible that anxiousness about meeting any one person is a sign that we have not yet reached "enlightenment"?

Preparation for the Week Ahead

Read John 13–17, then spend time this week thinking about how your prayer life matches up with John's instructions. Think about whether what you are doing is bringing glory to God and whether your prayer life is focused on you or on God's glory.

A Prayer for the Week Ahead

Father, I acknowledge that I don't even know how to pray. My prayer life is so selfish and so focused on me. Even when I am praying for other people, it's often a specific request for this or that rather than for the glory that can come to you through their circumstances. Show me how to pray first for your glory. Help me to bring my agenda in alignment with your greater vision. Show me where I am in disobedience so that I can be more in line with you and your teaching. I ask that the Holy Spirit bring me revelation so that I can access your wisdom. I attach myself to the vine of your strength, wisdom, and power. It is in Christ's name that I pray. Amen.

6

Golf Is a Contact Sport

PRINCIPLE 6: *Obey God. Abide in Christ.*

Whoever has my commands and obeys them, he is the one who loves me. He who loves me will be loved by my Father, and I too will love him and show myself to him. . . . If anyone loves me, he will obey my teaching. My Father will love him, and we will come to him and make our home with him.

—JOHN 14:21,23

As I write this part of the book, I'm in a chair with my leg in a cast. For 99.9 percent of you, I'm now the only guy you have heard about who broke his leg playing golf—and not as part of a cart accident. I've always said that if you're going to play anything, you might as well play hard. But that's not the whole story.

Last Sunday I was on my way to church when a friend called me to come play golf. I play with a great group of guys who like to get together on both Saturday and Sunday. I play Saturday when I can, but Sunday is my church time. This particular Sunday was a beautiful day in November, and my friend made the argument that it was probably the last nice day of the season. I could go to church all winter, he told me. He then promised that I could preach to the foursome if I came to play. I figured that was as good an excuse as any, so I turned around and headed off to the course.

I was having a great round and was only one over par after the front nine. My friend ended up being my cart partner, but he was not having quite the same round. He is due for a hip replacement in a few weeks, and it was getting the best of him. While teeing off on number ten, he had put two out of bounds. We drove down to where his balls had gone out of play. It was a side hill on pine straw, and I didn't want my friend to make the trek down the hill because of his hip, so I hopped out of the cart and went down to see if either ball had bounced back inbounds.

It turned out that the first ball had indeed hit a tree and bounced back in play. We both cheered, and I turned around to hunt for his second ball. At that moment, my left foot slipped on the pine straw and went straight up in the air. However, my right golf shoe caught some dirt and stuck in the ground. My body fell backward onto my right leg, and it folded over, snapping and ripping as it went. On my way down, I heard the crack, and then I felt the crack. Ouch!

After regrouping, I pulled my leg out from underneath my body. It's amazing how flexible your leg can be when you don't have those pesky little connecting bones keeping it straight. My friends went to call 911, but I refused to come off the course on a stretcher. We got back in the cart, and I had a wonderful ride back to the parking lot.

I say "wonderful ride" because, along the way, I passed out from the pain. I had never passed out before. Lots of pretty little floaty things dance around when you pass out. It was a very happy place—that is, until I woke up with my head in the lap of the driver of the cart. Now, several weeks later, we still haven't been able to make eye contact.

Later that afternoon, I had the first of two surgeries to pin my leg back together. It turned out that my friend was right: It was the last good golf day of the season. For me, it was the last good golf day for many months. And I've had plenty of time to reflect on a few life lessons:

1. Mom was right. Never listen to your friends. If they tell you to jump off a bridge, don't do it. If they tell you to come play golf on a Sunday, don't do it. I should have gone to church.

2. If your cart partner needs a hip replacement and hits two balls out of bounds, that's too bad. Let him get his own stupid balls. He deserves it.
3. Don't make God angry. That never ends well. Guess where I am every Sunday now.

Do I really think that God broke my leg? Of course not. But I do know that if I had been abiding in God's house, I would be running around my own house right now getting ready for Christmas. Instead, I'm on my backside in a cast for the next six weeks. There'll be a second surgery in three months to remove some of the screws. If I want the plate and pins removed, I'll need to have a third surgery in a year. I've got six months of rehab, and I'm told that my ankle will swell for the next two years. Just awesome!

As soon as I stepped out of God's path, I became subject to the fortunes of the world. My course correction was just a bit more dramatic than most. My big fall has given me a laugh-worthy way to reflect on living within God's plan. I now have a very physical reminder every minute of every day as to what it means to step outside of his plan. For that matter, so does my wife, who has to do every little thing for me. (You can only imagine how well that's going.)

A Very Clear Path

Despite this painful reminder, all I really needed to do was follow a clear road map laid out for all of us to help us stay within God's plan, which is especially clear in chapters 14–17 of the gospel of John. Did you read that passage, as I recommended in the previous chapter? If not, take some time to read it now, at least chapters 14–16. It's a short read, but it could change your view of how obedience can actually set us free.

I believe that most non-Christians and even new believers tend to think that obedience is limiting and all about drudgery and that being obedient is subservient and weak. Childhood was the time to obey a higher authority, but we're adults now, and we have the freedom to do whatever we please within the law. Why would we possibly want to adhere to some new, stricter set of rules and expectations now that we have the chance to do whatever we want?

The apostle John shows us why in his account of Jesus' teachings. If we abide in Christ and follow God's commands, we gain access to God's divine power through His Holy Spirit. How cool is it to think that if we follow what Christ commanded, the Holy Trinity will move in with us. Can you picture yourself living in a house with God, Christ, and the Holy Spirit? Talk about rubbing elbows with celebrities. Now that's a group I'd really want to have dinner with!

We can have that dream, but there's a twist. We have to step up first. God does not always act first and then we follow. When we act, God follows our action with his own. If we have faith, then God responds. If we listen to what Christ teaches, then Christ shows himself to us. Faith plus obedience plus action puts God to work, in effect giving him the go-ahead to live in and through us.

For years, I would end my prayers by saying, "In Christ's name we pray," and then I would wonder why my prayers were not answered. John tells us why. We need to abide in — this means to stand for, dwell within, and wait for — Christ, and we need to follow his commands, which means to love one another as he loves us. Then and only then can we ask for something in his name. We can't live however we wish and then pop in for a moment with God to ask him for our need of the week.

Abide first, ask second.

Once I finally saw this theme in the book of John, I began to realize that the concept shows up everywhere in the Bible. I happen to be reading the book of Daniel this week, and this principle shows up at least three times in the first five chapters. In this Old Testament narrative, Daniel and his three friends were in captivity in Babylon and were commanded to do things contrary to God's Law. They refused despite the threat of severe consequences. These three examples are:

1. Daniel refused to eat the food of his captors. After
   refusing — he took a stand — God then softened the heart

of the jailer, who gave Daniel and his friends a chance to test their own diet — God showed up. Before it was all over, the jailer saw that they were healthier than the other captives and allowed them to remain on the Jewish diet — God showed up again.

But Daniel resolved not to defile himself with the royal food and wine. . . . God had caused the official to show favor and sympathy to Daniel. (Daniel 1:8-9)

2. Daniel's three friends were told to worship a false idol, or they would be burned alive. They refused — they took a stand — and were thrown into the furnace. Yet they were completely unharmed in the fire — God showed up. The king called them out of the furnace and declared their God to be the mightiest of them all. The king then declared their religion to be sacrosanct and appointed them to a very high position in the government — God showed up yet again.

Praise be to the God of Shadrach, Meshach and Abednego, who has sent his angel and rescued his servants! They trusted in him and defied the king's command and were willing to give up their lives rather than serve or worship any god except their own God. (Daniel 3:28)

3. Later, a new king ordered the kingdom to pray to the golden idol. Daniel refused — he took a stand — and in the famous story he was thrown into the lion's den. He survived the night unharmed as God shut the mouths of the lions — God showed up. Daniel then became the king's greatest advisor — God showed up again.

I issue a decree that in every part of my kingdom people must fear and reverence the God of Daniel. (Daniel 6:26)

What Is God Waiting for You to Do?

God shows up when we abide in his Word and live his commands — even when things seem helpless. Another great example is Joseph, who as a teenager was sold into slavery in Egypt. Joseph stayed true to his faith even in very difficult circumstances. In the process, everything he touched flourished, and he ended up running the entire country, second only to Pharaoh.

So what is God waiting for us to do before he shows up at our work? Is he waiting for us to do what is right in the eyes of the Lord? How many little sacrifices do we make to our faith to stay in good graces with our employer? How many of us are worried about being fired or ostracized for not going along with the crowd?

God doesn't put many of us in life-and-death situations at work, but he does offer us hundreds or even thousands of little decisions over the course of our career that give us the opportunity to either show up for him or sacrifice our faith one little act at a time. If we are willing to stand up to those decisions, God will show up to create an even better outcome than our small sacrifice in values may have saved us in the short term.

A great contemporary example of such business integrity is the Chick-fil-A franchise. Its founder is a Christian who refuses to operate on Sunday, even at the cost of losing millions of dollars in business every Sunday that the restaurants are closed. Yet the business has grown to become the second-largest chicken franchise in the U.S., and the company has had forty-two consecutive years of positive sales growth.

When we place our trust in God, follow his Word, and abide in him, he moves into our lives and blesses our families, our friends, and our work. We gain access to everything that God has to offer. But the key is that we have to step up first. We have to seek him with all our heart, mind, body, and spirit. We have to demonstrate our trust in him and be willing to put things at risk. Then we get to ask for whatever we need. And then we put God to work.

For Reflection and Discussion

1. What does it mean to obey God?
2. Jesus says to follow his commands. What is his greatest commandment? Think about it, discuss it, and then look at John 13:34 and 1 John 3–4.
3. Would you be willing to put your life at risk in order to obey God? How about your job?
4. Have you been waiting for God to make the first move?
5. Have you or someone you know stepped up first and then seen God show up in miraculous ways?
6. Does God allow things like broken legs to happen to bring us into his will?
7. Would you be willing to lose millions of dollars in business every Sunday in order to keep the Sabbath holy?
8. Many men of the Bible stood up to kings, and God showed up in a very big way. Could you stand up to the president of your country, considering all the power that he has at his disposal? Picture yourself standing before the supreme ruler of your nation and saying no to a demand that would cause you to compromise your spiritual values.

Preparation for the Week Ahead

This week, pay attention to all of the ways that you tend to give in to the world. Notice how you justify the small actions that go against what you know to be right.

Think about the big moments as well — those times when you were put on the spot. How did you respond? Did you have to put anything at risk in order to do the right thing? Did you put your job at risk? How about your credibility as the world would view it? Did secular people think more or less of you because of how you responded to the big test?

A Prayer for the Week Ahead

God, most of us do not yet have the faith to step into the furnace and know that you would keep us unharmed. Most of us would succumb to the pressures of the prison guards or the rulers of our world. Give me the kind of confident, passionate heart that Daniel and his friends brought with them into their captivity in Babylon. Give me that strength, confidence, and trust in both the big decisions and the small decisions. I want to stand up for you. I delight when you respond to my small acts of obedience and accomplish the things I would have called impossible just moments before. I ask all of this in Christ's name. Amen.

7

Rosebud's a Killer

PRINCIPLE 7: *Trust God.*

But I trust in you, O LORD; I say, "You are my God." My times are in your hands; deliver me from my enemies and from those who pursue me.

— PSALM 31:14-15

Commit your way to the LORD; trust in him and he will do this: He will make your righteousness shine like the dawn, the justice of your cause like the noonday sun.

— PSALM 37:5-6

Trust in the LORD with all your heart and lean not on your own understanding.

— PROVERBS 3:5

It is better to take refuge in the LORD than to trust in man.

— PSALM 118:8

Before getting into the very serious subject of trust, let's take a brief interlude for me to share the story of the first two days of marriage to my wife of twenty-five years. I promise you, this detour will make sense eventually.

When Deborah and I got married, we first lived in Fort Lauderdale, Florida. In my attempt to be romantic and unique all at the same time, I decided that our honeymoon spot would be someplace exotic and cold rather than someplace tropical. After all, we lived in a warm climate and had the islands available to us almost every day of the year. So I booked a trip to Kitzbühel, Austria. We would learn to ski in the Alps and begin our marriage with a great adventure!

This was the first of many, many mistakes.

After an exhausting day of wedding fun, we hopped on a flight to Frankfurt, Germany, and landed sometime the next morning with very little sleep to speak of. We were supposed to be greeted by English-speaking tour guides, but no such luck. They had our itinerary as well as the logistics and directions to take us to our final destination. It was supposed to be a ninety-minute trip to our warm and comfortable ski lodge.

After sitting in baggage claim for about two hours, I left my new bride with our bags and went in search of information on how we could get to our final destination. I was able to slowly piece together that we could catch a bus to Vienna and then transfer to Kitzbühel. It would be a four-hour journey, but it would get us there eventually, and at this point that was all that mattered.

Excited to finally have an action plan, I started threading my way back to Deborah. What I did not realize was that baggage claim had recently been designated a secure area because a terrorist threat had put Frankfurt on lockdown. (To give you an indication of the level of tension at the time, there were tanks parked outside the terminal.)

I could not read any of the airport signs, and no one spoke English to help me find my way back into the secure area. When I saw a security guard leave baggage claim, I waited until he was looking the other way and slipped through the doors before they locked behind him. Quite pleased with myself, I smiled and proceeded toward the area where Deborah was waiting.

Just as I began walking in her direction, I heard the distinct sound of guns being cocked behind me. *"Achtung! Halt!"* more than one voice shouted. I don't speak German, but I've watched *Hogan's Heroes* enough to know that this is not a good thing to hear from behind you.

I raised my hands and turned around to see three young German soldiers pointing machine guns at my head. All shouted at me loudly in German. If it's possible, they were more nervous than I was. But because they had the guns, I got down on the ground and did my best to demonstrate the demeanor of a subservient puppy.

One put a gun to my head while another patted me down for weapons. The third gunman searched for my wallet. Unfortunately (an understatement to say the least), I didn't have any identification on me. I had given Deborah my travel portfolio, which contained the contents of my wallet, our tickets, my passport, and all the travel-related information we had. I was anonymous, and as far as my captors were concerned it was a sure sign that I was a terrorist.

One hour and two colonoscopies later, I was finally set free into baggage claim, where my new bride was slumped over a pile of bags in tears. Deborah had no idea where I'd been and had been panicked that something terrible had happened to me. I was thinking that she'd be extremely happy to see me, but this was total naïveté on the part of a day-old husband. She was infuriated. After the first of what would become many heated exchanges that day, we headed out to find our bus.

The bus ride was its own adventure, and we were relieved to finally arrive at the hotel, where we could get warm and even sleep for a couple of hours. But as we walked into the lobby, we discovered that it was actually colder inside the hotel than outside. Our hosts had used up their allotment of heating oil for the week, so there would be no hot water or heat for the next thirty-six hours.

How could we make the best of a crazy situation? Because we had not counted on all the travel delays, we decided to move directly into our first evening adventure—a candlelight bobsled run down a local mountain.

On the bus ride up the mountain, we were handed a release form. In the United States, these things are often three pages of fine print.

In Austria, it was one sentence that basically said, "We acknowledge that we will probably die tonight." At this point, death seemed like sweet relief, so we both signed and proceeded with our plans.

At the top of the mountain, they filled us with hot-spiced wine and, after a few glasses, we felt as if things might be looking up. Then they marched us outside and handed us our sleds. I was expecting an Olympic-style bobsled, but what they gave us was something similar to what I used back in the 1960s to sled down the little hill outside my house. In fact, I think my sled back then was bigger.

I laughed, but they didn't. They said something in German to each other and gestured us toward the hill. I asked them for the second sled for Deborah, but they replied that this sled was for both of us. I laughed again. They didn't laugh again. They just muttered something to each other in German and gestured us both toward the hill.

The only instruction we received was that if we wiped out, we needed to get off the track immediately because, thirty seconds behind us, another couple would be screaming down the hill at two hundred miles an hour on a sled made for children with blades that would slice you in half if they hit you at that speed.

Then they loaded us on the sled and, as they pushed us away, hollered at us to watch out for the ramp after the third candle. I turned around to ask, "What ramp?" but Deborah and I had already hurtled off into the darkness.

I was in front with my legs dangling out over the tiny sled. Deborah was in back with half of her rear end on the sled and the other half off the back of the sled, putting her latter half only a couple of inches above the ice. This created sparks as the buttons on her jeans grazed the ice during our downward plunge. While uncomfortable for Deborah, the sparks provided the only light on the mountain, and for that I was grateful.

We passed the first candle about two minutes into the run. I remember wondering why they called this a candlelight bobsled run. We were getting only three candles on an entire mountain, each providing about five seconds of dim light. We also didn't have an actual bobsled. We had a miniature version of Rosebud, the sled from the movie *Citizen Kane*. We had been sucked in by the propaganda of the travel agent. I thought, *Oh well. At least the legal release was truthful. Surely we will die tonight.*

We had long since stopped trying to control the sled and just acknowledged that we were at its mercy. We had approached terminal velocity by the second candle, but we were now laughing hysterically. By the time we got to the third candle, I had forgotten all about the warning of the ramp. Impending death has a way of getting you focused on the present moment like nothing else, and you tend to forget all worldly warnings and distractions.

But I would remember the ramp soon enough. It was the only thing that had light on it on the entire mountain, except for the hot-spiced wine house. The ramp was a twenty-foot wall positioned at nearly a ninety-degree angle to the direction we were currently heading in. I saw the light in the distance as the ramp quickly came into view.

I was later told that this obstacle was intended to slow us down gradually, but I'm not sure how approaching a wall angled at ninety degrees at two hundred miles an hour qualifies as gradual. My eyes grew very wide, and I dug my heels into the ice. In retrospect, I'm not sure how both of my legs didn't snap right off at the time. Behind me, Deborah started screaming in my ear. Between the sparks coming off her rear end and the ice particles flying into the air from my boots, we looked like the final act of the Ice Capades.

We hit that wall, which actually was slightly curved, and soared about fifteen feet up the embankment. Somewhere at the top of our arc, gravity took effect, and Deborah dropped off the back of the sled. (We later discovered that she literally broke her tailbone that night.) Eventually, Rosebud and I also returned to earth. We landed only about a foot to the right of Deborah as my head bounced off the icy floor.

Dazed, I looked up to see Rosebud continuing its way down the bobsled run, into the darkness. Deborah and I were sliding down the track as well, but then we hit a flat spot and stopped. Both of us were lying on our backs in the pitch black. I think we were both moaning, but I can't be sure. I do remember looking up and thinking how nice the stars looked in Austria. Or maybe it was heaven. I couldn't be sure about that either.

I could hear something off in the distance and at first thought that it might be angels. But then I recalled the first warning — "If you wipe out, get off the run immediately." I started yelling to my bride to wake up and get off the ice. She wouldn't move. I became more insistent, as I now clearly heard words hollered in delight by the couple flying down the track behind us. But Deborah would not move.

I got up to get to her but kept sliding. When I finally reached her, she was still not moving. I picked her up as best I could, slipped and slid over to the wall of the bobsled run, and threw her over the wall. I could hear the thud of my bride landing in the snow. But I also could hear the blades on the ice of the couple behind us. I couldn't see them, but I knew that they and Rosebud's younger brother were barreling in my direction.

I finally leapt over the wall, feeling the *whoosh* of their sled as they flew by. I landed somewhere near Deborah. We did not move. We did not speak. I'm not sure if we were even breathing. It seemed as though five minutes passed with no sound. And then Deborah said something that still haunts me to this day. Out of the darkness, in the still of the night, with nothing but God and the stars surrounding us, I heard her say, "The honeymoon's over!"

Remember, the honeymoon had not even begun. From the instant we were pronounced husband and wife until this very moment, we had been on planes, trains, automobiles, and Rosebud. Our hotel room was twenty-two degrees Fahrenheit, and we had done little more than move our bags into our room before heading to the bobsled run. So this was not a good thing for a newly married man to hear.

But the rest of the trip was even more bizarre. Our room was haunted by a cigar-smoking ghost (or at least that's what Deborah said); there was an active bowling alley right below our room; and the ski instructor we booked for a week spent the entire time trying to get my wife to run off with him. It was perhaps the wackiest honeymoon ever and an inauspicious way to start our marriage.

A Not-So-Humorous Journey

This long story is meant to illustrate that life is crazy. Things don't work out as you plan. Stuff happens. The pudding hits the fan, and people get messy. And while the example I've shared is hopefully a bit humorous to you, there are also plenty of examples in life that are not quite so humorous. We all have stuff that can come along and dramatically change everything. We have our stuff, and you have your stuff.

In our case, most of our next twenty-five years turned out to be what most would consider a hard life. Our youngest daughter, Amanda, was diagnosed with cancer at a very young age. By age six, she had survived cancer three times. By age eighteen, she had endured more than one hundred and twenty-five surgeries, including two liver transplants. She's had her eardrums reconstructed twice and is now quite deaf without hearing aids. We're still dealing with late-term effects of the physical and emotional impact of a childhood that entailed at least five death sentences.

You might imagine that during that time I developed quite a trust issue with God. I prayed to him again and again but seemingly to no avail. I poured my heart out night after night and sometimes all night. But I got no answer. I never stopped believing in him—that would have been easy. I knew he was there. The hard, painful part for me was the apparent silence from heaven, which made me wonder if God didn't care or if he was deliberately causing this to happen. Neither option was a valid one for me. I grew bitter and came to believe that God cannot be trusted. (Our journey is chronicled in my earlier book, *Amanda's Gift*.)

While the issues that led to my lack of trust might have been more tangible to me than for some other people, I guarantee that we all have trust issues. Do you trust God—I mean, totally, unconditionally, completely, no matter what the circumstances? Most of us have never really thought it through, or we *think* we trust God, but our trust has never gone up against a serious test. To see what I mean, grade yourself honestly against the following criteria. I confess that I have personally failed every one of these situations many times:

- I never, ever feel anxious about anything because I know that God will fix every problem in every situation.
- I give away everything I have because I know that God will meet my needs tomorrow.
- I never worry about the future.
- I never feel the need to plan for the future because I know God will bring me exactly what I need exactly when I need it.
- I never worry about the things I did today.
- I never worry about what people think of me.
- I have total confidence that I'm going to heaven.
- I never feel condemned.
- I never get upset about a situation at work because I know that God will fix it for me.
- I would have no concern if someone held a gun to my head or came to attack my family.
- Once I pray, I stop thinking about my problems because I know that God has my back.

The list could go on, but I hope this little exercise helped you to get a better glimpse of your true level of trust in God. We're human; we all fall short of complete trust in our Lord. In fact, I'd be willing to bet that most of us trust a spouse, friend, or family member more than we trust God. And that, my friend, is the reason why many of us do not receive answers to our prayers. It's why many of us struggle from day to day, whether at work or at home. Unmitigated trust in our heavenly Father is a fundamental part of the prayer equation.

Jesus taught that if we have faith (trust) the size of a tiny mustard seed, we can tell a mountain to move from here to there, and it will do as we say (see Matthew 17:20). The converse of his statement is that *if we don't have at least that level of faith, then the mountain isn't going anywhere.* And when the mountain doesn't move, we get frustrated, sad, and angry. It's a vicious spiral downward into despair, wondering why God doesn't hear us. I have spent far too much time in that place.

It's Easier to See the Big Stuff

While I eventually started to see how my trust issues were weakening me in the face of my *big* problem (my daughter's health), I was missing the point in the hundreds of small problems I encountered every day — everything from difficult customers to problem employees to the guy who cut me off in traffic. Every day, all day, you and I have a series of little mountains standing in our way, and we fail to see that we have more control over our circumstances than we think.

God gives us hundreds, maybe thousands, of opportunities daily to move mountains. When I finally started to get it, I began the adventure of regarding these problems *not as annoyances but as opportunities* to grow in my faith and to watch God at work. I can testify that it has become almost fun to see how quickly problems get resolved now that I understand the faith dynamic that's in play.

I'm thinking of a situation that took place many years ago with a $30 million customer our company had struggled with for several years. No matter what we did, these people seemed determined to be unhappy. If we fixed a perceived problem, they found something else to complain about. When they ran out of problems, they hired consultants to review our operations and unearth more perceived problems.

This cycle continued for five years. During that time, many of us canceled vacations at the last minute to try to resolve this customer's issues. It was not uncommon to schedule meetings or conference calls before 6 a.m. to discuss how we would engage the client that day or after 10 p.m. to debrief how our recent action plan worked in meeting their needs the previous afternoon. If hundreds of jobs had not been on the line, I would have resigned from this account long ago. But jobs were indeed on the line, so we continued to deal with these people's irrational behavior.

During that turbulent five years, they put their business out to bid multiple times. But we kept winning the business back because we had the best deal on the table. When they put their business out for bid the fourth time, a competitor submitted a proposal saying that they could save the customer millions of dollars. We knew the numbers were incorrect and protested the bid.

The relationship got mired in a legal mess. More than once I reconciled myself to just letting our competitor have the business even though theirs was a faulty proposal. But as I'd pray about it, something inside kept telling me to stick with it. The legal battle went on for nearly a year. It was exhausting. I kept praying and thinking, *Surely this can't be what you want, God.* But I kept getting the message to be persistent.

Then one morning the message evolved. I normally get up very early and use that time to read, pray, and just relax into God. On this day I was up extra early and was able to do all of that and still take the dog for a long walk. As usual, Max was running wild, excited to be out and about in the morning air. While walking behind him in the dark, I silently prayed about a number of issues, including this customer. I asked God again whether it was right to keep going or if we should just give in, take our losses, and move on.

This is one of the many times that I was working on my trust issues with God. And because I had the strong feeling deep inside that I should stick with the battle, I didn't want to give up if God was wanting me to stay faithful. But I also didn't want to be ungodly by protracting a legal battle that was ruining the lives of all the people involved. I was very confused as to what was the right path, the godly path.

That's when a new revelation struck me. I can't say it was as clear as the message I had received in my basement, but on this crisp morning walk with my dog I got another very strong message, a very lucid thought that stood way out from my normal mental chatter.

If I deliver this account to you, will you trust in me?

I was a little stunned by the question. "Of course I will," I said out loud. "I'll also trust in you if you don't deliver the account. But if you want to deliver the account, that would be splendid."

When I "woke up" from that conversation, Max had stopped in front of me and was looking back as if to ask what on earth I was doing. I was stopped in the street, talking out loud. I looked around to see if any neighbors were awake and peering outside. Fortunately, they were not. We walked home in silence as I contemplated yet another amazing spiritual experience.

Over the next six months, the actual events that occurred with this account were not quite as clear as the message I had received that morning. On several occasions it appeared that we had lost the battle. This account was not just on life support—it was dead. Gone. I remember praying something to the effect of, "That's okay, Lord. I'm sure I did something wrong here. No problem. Thanks anyway."

But each time the account seemed to go away, something happened, and we would be back in the game. Difficult people at the account would quit. Lawyers would change. Enemies suddenly became champions. But just as our hopes would rise, something bad would happen, and the cycle would start all over again. The contract would appear dead in the water, then it would miraculously return to life. We rode this roller coaster at least six or seven times.

But something was happening inside *me*. As I daily sought God's guidance and watched him work, this difficult customer ceased feeling like a thorn in my side. Instead, they were a source of joy! It was exciting to anticipate what would happen next. I couldn't wait for the day when we could announce that we had retained the business.

But that's *not* what happened.

The lawsuit was arbitrated, and we actually lost the business. It was indeed over. I was completely deflated. All of that anticipation, all of that hope, all of the faith I had built up was shot. I just couldn't believe it. Clearly I had misunderstood the message from God.

I wondered if perhaps this was a test for me to keep my trust in God despite the outcome. I did my best to hold on to some of that lesson.

Still, I could not help but feel let down. I pretended to trust, but in reality I lost what little trust I had. In the months that followed, I kept a stiff upper lip but lost my sense of wonder and excitement over the stuff that happened every day. I forgot about trusting God. I didn't stop trusting him; I simply forgot to even think about it.

In the days following the announcement of arbitration, we tried to figure out how to fill the hole left in our budget by this loss of $30 million. It was a struggle, and we knew that on the day they left us we would fall behind in so many important ways. People would have to be fired. Bonuses would be lost. We would let our company down. Although I never said the words out loud, I was thinking, *See, I told you so. Don't trust God because he can't be trusted. He doesn't really answer prayer.*

But that's not the end of the story.

As we worked to unwind our legal situation, it turned out that the customer owed us a considerable sum for breaching the contract. The amount of the settlement was actually more than the profit we would have made from this customer in eighteen months — more than enough to help us make budget for the year.

It also turned out that our competitor could not move fast enough to take over this customer by the agreed-upon date. So we got three extra months of business that we thought had been lost. Then, on the day we left the account, the customer announced that they were in dire financial need and had only ten days of cash on hand. The CEO resigned, and the place went into chaos.

As our competitor took over the account, it proved to be too much for them. They couldn't run the business properly, so they started pulling resources from their other customers in the area. As these other customers saw their resources go away, they became angry and approached us to take over their business. These new customers were better partners and more profitable in aggregate than the customer we had lost.

I later flew back into the city where this difficult ex-customer was based. I felt a complete sense of relief to visit with our new clients, who wanted to talk about strategic ways to improve our partnership rather than all the transactional ways we could argue about the business. It became fun to do business again in that city, and our numbers eventually grew to be better than before.

This definitely was not the way I would have envisioned having the account delivered to me. It was far better! I had trusted in God to show me the way and had given him enough room to work his blessings in a manner that I could never have imagined on my own. It was an awesome experience. It invigorates me to this day and gives me tangible proof that God can be trusted when I have the faith to put him to work. Since that time, I have had three similar situations in which the account was eventually resolved in a way I never could have expected.

We will have tribulations in this world. Jesus said so according to John 16:33. But he also said that we should be of good cheer because he has overcome the world. These tribulations are our opportunity to trust in God whether they are small problems or large and whether they are emotionally distressing trials or comical circumstances at which we can look back and laugh.

In Matthew 6:33, Jesus said, "Seek first his kingdom and his righteousness, and all these things will be given to you as well." Trust in God is an inner confidence and faith that, no matter what circumstances we are going through at the time, God has our best interests at heart and will lead us through the wilderness — in a way and time that he knows is best for us. There will be plenty of times when you will think you have failed or that God has let you down. It's sometimes part of the learning process. My account problem did not resolve overnight. It took months, and I had many moments in which I doubted God. My daughter's health issues were twenty years in the making, and they created a lot of heartache and disappointment in my relationship with God. But all of these circumstances have brought me to a place of trust that I never would have attained without them.

Take stock of your trust level. See how you can put your faith in a God who wants only what is best for you in the long run. That does not imply that it will all feel good at the time. But it does offer a long-term peace that surpasses all understanding.

For Reflection and Discussion

1. What does it mean to trust someone?
2. Is God really to be trusted?
3. Why does Christ say that in this world bad things will happen? Why can't things be good all the time?
4. Is it possible to develop trust with someone (or God) if you've never been put into a situation in which trust was needed and demonstrated?
5. Have you ever trusted someone you've never met, like someone you've only talked to on the phone or the Internet or seen on TV?
6. Are you willing to accept the struggle that comes along with your faith journey, or would you rather things be comfortable for now?
7. When things are really bad and appear impossible, how would the world view someone who still believed in the promised outcome?
8. If you are sick, can you trust God to heal you? If so, would that be every time or only when it's in your best interests?
9. Do you trust someone more on earth than you trust God? Who is it and why?
10. Would you trust God to save you if you were thrown into a lion's den or a fiery furnace?

Preparation for the Week Ahead

Consider the many mountains in front of you this week. How could you turn these big and small problems over to God and trust that he will resolve them in due time? Notice what happens when you trust him. How does it make you feel? Are you willing to give God a chance to turn the hard things into opportunities rather than problems?

A Prayer for the Week Ahead

Father, if I was completely honest with myself, I'd admit that I don't trust you. I know in my head that you are good and that you want the best for me, but most of the time that thought doesn't translate into my everyday life. I think I need to fix the problems, I think I need to solve the puzzles, and I think that there's no way you'd step in and catch me when I fall. That stuff only happens in Bible stories from thousands of years ago. There's no way you'd do it now.

But how can I say you are my God and not trust in that? How can I see all the loving things you have done and not have a faith that can move mountains? How can I say I am yours but then act as though you are not there, active in my life?

I remember that during the Exodus from Egypt, the people saw pillars of smoke during the day and fire that guided them by night. They saw you part the sea. They saw manna fall from heaven. And they still didn't trust you. We are often a weak-minded people. I confess that sin before you.

I do not want to resign myself to a life filled with confusion or fear or doubt. I will continually seek your presence. I will wait to feel you move in me and know that I have a God in my life who can do anything, even the impossible. I will trust in that . . . until the next time I don't. But then I will repent and trust you again until it becomes who I am.

Guide me on this journey, and make yourself known to me as I struggle with insecurity so that I might be bold and confident in your presence and in your grace. It is in Christ's name that I pray. Amen.

"She's Touching Me!"

PRINCIPLE 8: *Yield to attack.*

Do not take revenge, my friends, but leave room for God's wrath,
for it is written: "It is mine to avenge, I will repay," says the Lord.
— ROMANS 12:19

When Deborah and I got married, the car I brought into the marriage was a Mazda RX7. I loved that car. It was sporty, it was fast, and it was cool.

It only had two seats, so when the time came for our first child to be born, I went out to buy a more family-friendly car without telling Deborah so that it would be a big, happy surprise.

I showed up at the house thinking my bride was going to be so proud of me for giving up the last vestige of my single life by becoming a responsible husband with the practical car. She happened to be outside when I arrived . . . and as I pulled into the driveway, she looked at me with complete disgust.

"What have you done?" she shrieked. This was not quite the reaction I was looking for.

On the list of her many complaints was that the back seat was obviously too small; when we had our second child, the kids would be able to touch each other.

"Who cares if they can touch each other?" I asked. "I never had problems with that growing up. My older sister is a saint. She treated me like a king, and we never had problems in the car."

Deborah had a different perspective. I'd see when the time came, she assured me.

As it turns out, the car worked just fine for our oldest. Even when our youngest arrived, the car worked well for about a year. But as both of them grew older, they began to bicker from the back seat. Then came that fateful day when the words were first uttered: "She's touching me!"

Although it had been three years since Deborah had made the comment about the back seat, we both immediately turned and looked at each other. But it was too late. We were locked into that car for at least another thirty-six easy payments.

The gradual escalation of the conflict that followed was something to behold. The mild complaints about touching turned into temper tantrums and eventually punching, kicking, biting, and scream-ing—and that was just between Deborah and me. But seriously, I can remember checking my rearview mirror and seeing arms, legs, and small pets flying around the back seat at any given time. No matter how many times they were punished, the dynamic between my two daughters continued, even into their twenties.

She's Touching Me, Version 2.0

While both of my girls would now acknowledge their backseat behavior as childish, it's not all that different from how things sometimes work in the business world. Somebody says something that offends another person in a meeting, and the offended one simmers until the next meet-ing when he or she can toss a pithy comment back at the first person. If the corporate culture is not designed to contain it, these casual com-ments can turn into energy-consuming conflict, gossip, and infighting.

It's natural to have competition in the workplace, and not all compe-tition is a bad thing. Healthy competition fuels innovation and success. If two people compete over the top spot in a company, it's going to make both of them operate at the highest possible level. If two companies fight over a customer, it will make them more efficient and more creative in their offerings. Competition and conflict can motivate us to excellence.

Indeed, constructive company cultures encourage diversity of thought to fuel positive competition and better output. A little passionate disagreement at times can lead to a far better product than always agreeing about everything. A high-performance team not only allows for the occasional disagreement but might even encourage it as long as it is also capable of resolving those differences over time.

So this chapter is not intended to imply that all conflict is bad and that we should always avoid confrontation. Occasionally, a company or an individual will need to stand its ground in order to live by its principles or advance a righteous cause. We operate in a sinful world, and occasionally we need to stand up to that sin. As we learned earlier, Jesus Christ was not shy about confronting hypocrisy and evil. But his enduring good news is that love should replace hate and forgiveness should replace revenge.

To prove his point, Jesus allowed a sinful people to torture and crucify him when with one word he could have wiped them all out and sent them straight to hell. Amazingly, his response to their unjust attack was to ask God to forgive them. He lived his commandment to love our enemies, which gave his words credibility, strength, and power. He walked the talk.

If Christ could forgive the men who murdered him, then why can't I be more loving with people who simply annoy me? As a follower of Christ, I'm called to a more compassionate response to the way my competitors, coworkers, and customers treat me every day. I'm called to think differently when tribulations, both big and small, present themselves in my life as drama, conflict, and emotional or physical pain.

Creating Attack

I'm not exactly a stellar example of yielding to attack. I'm embarrassed at times about how much of an aggressor I can be. I'm a ten out of ten when it comes to competitiveness. I've taken many business personality profiles over my career, and I am always in the top 1 percent of competitive groupings. In many ways this determination has led to my success, but I can see how it has also stunted my growth as a leader, as a friend, and as a family man.

For much of my life I was the kind of driver who raced up behind you in the left lane and tailgated you, even though there was room to pass in the right lane. I thought it was my duty to teach you a lesson about how slower drivers should keep right. And when you finally moved over, I would accelerate alongside you and stare over at you just to make sure you got the point.

If you played any sport with me, I'd be all over you about the right way to play the game. In business, I aggressively followed both internal and external competition to see how I stacked up. If I was ahead of you, I'd make sure you knew it. If I was behind, I was convinced you were either gaming the system or just lucky that month.

As I matured over time, the gamesmanship turned to more "acceptable" forms of aggressiveness—at least as the world would view it. If a competitor took business from me, I would attack them at three of their accounts. If someone did us an injustice, I would take the matter into legal proceedings. If someone hurt my kids, I'd make sure the culprits got into big trouble.

I could justify these counterattacks as not only acceptable in the world but as something expected of me as a leader. We live in a secular world in which sometimes a bully only stops being a bully when he or she gets beaten in a fair fight. Sometimes competition stops coming after you only when they realize that they will pay a steep price for doing so.

In modern times, we've seen this play out with a cadre of CEOs who have been summarily dismissed, exiled, or imprisoned. These men and women were initially lauded in their careers for being strong, aggressive, and successful. Many became very rich and won against the "nice guys"—for a time. Yet in the end they were found to be corrupt, destructive, or incompetent.

Good stewards, by contrast, are in it for the long haul. They are willing to absorb short-term attacks and setbacks in order to maintain a strong foundation built upon values, principles, and truth. They would rather lose an account than win or maintain it with a false set of assumptions or promises. They understand that sometimes it's harder *not* to react than it is to lash out in anger or revenge. Again, think of Jesus during his beatings and crucifixion. It would have been much easier, humanly speaking, for him to wipe out his accusers and assailants or to come down from the cross as his mockers taunted him to do. He could have, but that would not have fulfilled God's plan.

A Vengeful God?

My aggressive streak continued for decades. But as I got deeper into the New Testament, I started to question my behavior. The more I studied, prayed, and contemplated, the more I realized that Christ was not especially pleased with my extreme competitiveness. That bothered me. But it wasn't until I delved more deeply into the Old Testament that I finally got a glimpse of what God was looking to do with me on this issue.

One day the phrase "Vengeance is mine; I will repay, saith the Lord" (Romans 12:19, KJV) appeared in my New Testament reading, and it stayed with me. I'm not sure why, but it just kept nagging at me. Everywhere I turned, the phrase kept coming up. I couldn't shake loose of it, and I couldn't understand why God wanted to be vengeful if Christ was teaching us to be forgiving. So I went back into the Old Testament to explore where the phrase originated.

The saying comes from Deuteronomy 32:35. In this part of the Old Testament, Moses sang a song to Israel just before his death in order to pass along the Law to a people accustomed to oral tradition. "Vengeance is mine; I will repay, saith the Lord" is then repeated in the New Testament letters to the Romans and Hebrews so that we know it's an important, timeless point worthy of our examination.

But even after months of thinking about it, I still couldn't seem to reconcile with this direction from God. I've always been more a fan of the God of the New Testament than the God of the Old Testament, mostly because I don't understand all the violence in the Old Testament. It bothers me. I don't like it, and I can't justify it. I know he's the same God in both testaments, and I'm praying about that, but I still lack understanding and insight into what was going on back in those earlier days of history.

So when I first heard the phrase "Vengeance is mine," I just dismissed it as part of that Old Testament hard-line stuff. But through an insight that I know originated with the Holy Spirit within me, I developed a new perspective on the statement. *God is not saying that he wants vengeance because he's a vengeful God. He's saying that we, his people, are not to be vengeful.* He's saying that if a wrong needs to be made right, *he* will take care of it for us. *He* will do the dirty work, leaving us free to be peaceful, loving, and forgiving—which, when you think about it, sets us *free*, period. We are free of debilitating hate and resentment, free of energy-draining demands for justice or revenge, and free of the need to spread poor-me stories of how awful the offender is.

God wants to handle the defeat or the injustice so that you and I can be *free*.

This realization completely changed my paradigm. It also became the only way that I could begin to rid myself of my desire to have other people pay a price for doing me wrong. If I at least had confidence that my enemies would get theirs, then I could feel satisfied that justice eventually would be done. I could release all the negative energy I was burning up thinking about how to get back at them. If vengeance was needed, it was up to God, not to me.

The Real Anger-Management Solution

In retrospect, I began to see how this principle had worked in one particular situation that had overwhelmed me for almost a year. A young man had hurt our family deeply, and I just couldn't let it go. He had caused us deep emotional, physical, and financial pain. To make matters worse, he was proud of what he had done. He had not even a speck of remorse over it.

I would lie awake at night thinking about how to get back at him. Terrible things crossed my mind. I'd think about it before I went to bed. I'd think about it when I woke up. I'd think about it at work. As months passed, I had pretty much become the embodiment of anger. I was seething nearly every minute of the day. My obsession carried over into my work and family relationships. When all that you think about is anger and revenge, there isn't room for much else.

One evening, I could not take it anymore. I got down on my knees and finally turned my bitterness over to God. I had not yet even noticed the phrase "Vengeance is mine," but I had to believe that God could handle this injustice better than I could. I was being destroyed by the hatred and vengeful thoughts that consumed me. After turning the situation over to God, I felt peace for the first time in a very long while.

A few weeks later, this man was arrested for something else and spent more than a year in the justice system. I hear that he has turned his life around, and I am sincerely happy about that. Had I gone after him, I would have only messed up his life worse than it already was, and along the way I might have done something very, very stupid to ruin my own life and my family's life. I could not handle my need for revenge in a constructive way, but God could. He solved both my problem and the offender's problem.

In the process, I came to realize just how much time and energy I had invested in slow burns over what other people had done to me. Upon reflection, I learned that much of my personality and character were being built *not* upon who I wanted to be but upon my reaction to what other people did and how they interacted with me. If they were nice, I was nice. If they were mean, I was mean. If they were aggressive, I was aggressive. If they got in my way, I got them out of my way.

None of this was serving me well, and it surely was not serving well the people who interacted with me. If I was nice, it was only because they behaved well enough to "deserve" niceness from me. And if I was angry or mean, it was because I felt that someone's angry attitude deserved a similar response.

The problem was that when I perceived that others mistreated me or someone I cared about, I didn't exactly model Christlike love to them in return. I modeled how the world reacts to tense situations — with aggression. So I actually became part of the problem. I displayed more of an ego-protective response than a Christlike response. I helped escalate rather than defuse the tension, which is the polar opposite of what good leadership is all about. I was more like a child, lashing out because someone had taken my toy or my date or my job or my peace. I was an adult version of "She's touching me!"

When I began to see this, I started trying to yield to attack — to let the big and small things go. While I still drive my car with a sense of urgency, I yield to those who don't have quite the same passion I do about getting from point A to point B. I haven't glared at people who drive me crazy on the road for about five years now. I don't feel constantly compelled to prove my point (although admittedly I'm still working on that one).

I'm okay now with letting other people win an argument even when I know they don't have all their facts straight. I no longer care if I don't get the credit for something insightful I've said or something positive I've done. But all of this was only possible after I acknowledged intellectually that God will make everything right in the end.

There's a simple saying that packs a powerful theological message: *Let go and let God*. In five simple words, that sums up a major principle of success that resonates throughout the Bible. The apostle Peter put it this way: "'God opposes the proud but gives grace to the humble.' Humble yourselves, therefore, under God's mighty hand, that he may lift you up in due time. Cast all your anxiety on him because he cares for you" (1 Peter 5:5-7).

When I started obeying that biblical imperative, I began to feel free from the oppressive bondage of extreme competitiveness, anger, and vengefulness. This was a huge step for me because it ran counter to all my natural tendencies. I still have to work at it, with God's help. But it's made a world of difference already.

Love Our Enemies?

It was then that my heart and mind were opened to a better understanding of what Jesus meant when he commanded us to love our enemies, a concept I never understood in worldly terms.

Once I had God's word on it that he would eventually take care of whatever vengeance was due and that he would "lift [me] up in due time," I was freed to release thoughts of vengeance from my *mind*, which gave me the space and the strength to release them from my *heart* as well. I have to admit that the transformation didn't happen overnight; in fact, it was gradual, consisting of steps forward and backward over many years. But I can tell you that as a result I began to see how loving an enemy would be possible.

I've still got a long way to go, especially as this relates to how I lead in a secular world. But the principle of yielding to attack (by controlling your response and trusting God with the situation) is gradually working its way into my daily mind-set. I can happily report to you that my inner world is becoming a far more peaceful place. When my competitors cheat to win an account, or when people act in an unethical manner, I take it to God in prayer and release it to his greater wisdom. He shows me the way when I put him to work, and I'm becoming a stronger, wiser, more effective leader as a result. I'm not there yet, but I'm better than I was.

This works in both big things and small things. When people do something that I don't agree with, or when the wait staff at a restaurant is rude, or when people in general do things that annoy me, I simply tell myself, "He is not my enemy." If there is a wrong to be righted, it doesn't belong to me. It belongs to God.

Instead of building a big emotional case in my mind, I'm learning to release perceived offenses, which frees me to model better Christlike behavior. But the reality is that I forget this principle often—and I mean often. At least three or four times a day, I start thinking about a perceived injustice done to me by this or that person. I start mulling over what I should've said and rehearsing what I ought to say next time. My mind races with thoughts of putting this person in his or her place. It's not a pretty sight, and it feels even worse inside as bitterness dampens my spirit. But then I realize what I'm doing, and I chuckle, sometimes aloud. *There I go again*, I acknowledge. Grateful that God's Holy Spirit has caught my attention, I thank God for reminding me to *let go and let God*, and I say a prayer for the person I was fussing about.

Does this principle work at home as well? While you might not consciously think of your children, your spouse, or your extended family as enemies, there might be times when you act as if they are! Teenage children can drive parents bonkers, and if you find yourself constantly complaining about them, then you're making them into an enemy whether you realize it or not. And if you blame your parents or your spouse or your in-laws for this or that in your life, you are also making them into an enemy — someone to blame for your ills. Instead of feeding the fight, try yielding to attack by releasing all frustration, resentment, and anger to God, trusting him to help you "love your enemies" and be a healing agent in these tense relationships.

The Time to React

Lest you think I've gone totally soft, now is a good time for the requisite, all-important caveat: In no way am I proposing that you and I should never stand up for what is right.

The apostle Paul demanded his rights as a Roman citizen, appealing from court to court until he got the audience he demanded. Martin Luther King Jr. stood up to gross injustice time and time again. Gandhi took on the entire British Empire to secure the rights of his people. Jesus took on the Sadducees and Pharisees directly and firmly.

There are times to take on the bullies. There are times to take on the hypocrites. There are times to stand up to injustice and evil. As British statesman and philosopher Edmund Burke said, "The only thing necessary for the triumph of evil is for good men to do nothing."

But it's what we do, how we do it, and under whose direction we proceed that matters. God might indeed use us to defend the defenseless or to stamp out evil, but it should be at his direction and with his help.

More often than not, God will not require tough action on your part. He'll simply resolve your problem for you in some peaceful way and in his own time. In Genesis 13, we see how God worked for Abram in a situation involving his nephew Lot. Abram had adopted Lot and taken care of him during the boy's childhood. God blessed them both, and they enjoyed so much abundance that their cattle were eating up all the fertile land. It became clear that one of them would have to take his household and cattle elsewhere in order for both to continue to thrive.

You'd think that Abram would easily win the question of who moves. He was, after all, the older and wealthier person. Abram had made sacrifices to care for Lot. You'd think that Lot would just acquiesce and say, "Thanks, Uncle Abram, I'll go find my way, and you stay here. You've been great!" But Lot did not do the right thing. He wanted to be the one to stay put.

Abram, on the other hand, took the high road. He said something along these lines: "Look, you and I are family. I don't want to fight about this. Look around, then take what you want. If you go left, then I'll go right. If you go right, then I'll go left. Whatever you want, I'll take what's left over. Choose, and I'll head in the opposite direction."

In those days, people lived or died depending on the land and water supply. For Abram to offer this was more than generous; in fact, from the world's perspective it was actually quite foolish. Lot couldn't believe his good fortune. He looked around and saw that the plain of Jordan was lush, green, fertile, and well-watered. It was an easy choice. He said, "I'll take this." Abram would be moving to land not nearly as good as what he gave his nephew.

But did Abram complain, stew, or aim to teach his uppity nephew a lesson? No. He released it all to God. He moved his family and flocks and herds to another land and built an altar to the Lord in gratitude for what he did have. Note that Abram expressed gratitude, not vengeance or bitterness, toward his selfish nephew. He trusted God to "lift [him] up in due time" and make him prosperous despite what his eyes saw before him.

And prosper he did, becoming the father of many nations.

Lot, on the other hand, went through tribulations. He lived in a wicked land. On the night that Sodom and Gomorrah were destroyed, he had to flee with his family. His wife disobeyed God's instruction, gazed back at the burning cities, and so was turned into a big salt lick. God had addressed the injustice "in due time," giving Abram what he deserved and Lot what he deserved.

By yielding to attack before the situation escalated to confrontation, Abram was blessed with peace and abundance. Instead of contending that he had every right to stay where he was as patriarch in the family, he yielded humbly and went his way, casting all anxiety on God. Furthermore, he bore no bad feelings. He displaced grousing with gratitude.

I must admit that I would not have been as gracious as Abram, which is, no doubt, why I'm often stuck in place. I would have said, "Hey, kiddo, this is my land. I took you in and cared for you rather than let you hit the streets. Now that you have abundance, you go make your own way out there in the real world and do the hard work that I had to do in order to get here. *Capice*? Now beat it."

Then I would have told the story to all my friends: "Can you believe how selfish kids are these days? I took this kid in when his dad died, and now he wants *my* land. What nerve! He says he's going to come get me and take my land. I'll show him. Just let him come. I'll be ready. I'll be waiting and show that spoiled brat what he has coming to him."

Does any of that sound similar to the dialogue going on in your head? Take any confrontation you've had recently, and I can promise that some version of this conversation is going on, whether with yourself, your kids, your spouse, your coworkers, or the guy in the next car over.

Just this week, despite all I've been learning, I found myself bashing a particular group that had done our company an injustice. The moment

I said it, I realized what a mistake I had made. But then I said it again. And then I said it a *third* time. Each time I realized what I was doing: In bashing the group, I was not loving my enemy or trusting God to take care of the situation.

Complaining about injustice is not the conversation that Christ wants us to have. As we've seen, Jesus is both counterintuitive and countercultural. He doesn't want us to bash—he wants us to bless. He wants us to trust that if a person deserves justice, God will take care of it in due time. Jesus wants us to release our anger and bitterness and actually pray for the person who drives us crazy. He wants us to love that person. See how Jesus said it directly: "You have heard that it was said, 'Love your neighbor and hate your enemy.' But I tell you: Love your enemies and pray for those who persecute you, that you may be sons of your Father in heaven" (Matthew 5:43-45).

Huh? That sounds nice—if you live in a convent. But that's not how it works in the real world. Out here, nice guys get crushed. Meekness is weakness. If I don't punch back, I'll just get punched again. If I don't attack first, that'll just give them more time to build a case against me. If I don't crush them, they will crush me. If I don't outperform them, I'll lose my job.

But it's that very thought process that Jesus challenges. It's that kind of inner dialogue that he wants us to release. He doesn't want us plotting revenge or wishing something bad on someone or planning someone's demise. He wants us blessing and praying for everyone regardless of what they have done for us or not done for us. He doesn't say, "Love your enemy unless, of course, he's been a real jerk." He says, "Love your enemy." Period.

When we obey this command, we release our anger, bitterness and anxiety, all of which have been proven to cause debilitation and disease. We relate from a perspective of love, calmness, and strength with everyone around us at work and at home. People sense that strength and respond accordingly.

By becoming weaker, we actually become stronger.

Yielding at Work

I'm seeing this principle work again and again.

In one instance, we had a $12 million account that decided to put our business out to bid. A competitor underbid us by a considerable amount, saying that they could consolidate services and remove considerable overhead. We had been running the business for years, and we knew that those savings were not available, but the customer bought the story.

We were very upset. We knew that the competitor could not deliver what they promised, yet we were losing a long-term client to this lie. We burned about it. We thought about throwing any number of people under the bus in order to demonstrate that we were right. But that was not who we were. Finally, we wished our customer and competitor well and made a graceful, professional exit. I personally released it to God and moved on.

We didn't realize it, but the situation turned bad for this competitor immediately. In order to hit their ridiculously low numbers, the first thing they announced was a massive layoff. Then they cut the salaries and benefits of all our former associates. They brought in very strict policies so they could cut labor and material costs, all of which dramatically impacted customer service. It was a mess.

Within three months, our former client called us back in for a meeting. Within six months, we were back running the facility. Our client was so pleased to have us back that they later served as a reference for us when the competitor made outrageous claims to other clients of ours about what they could do to reduce cost. The competitor finally backed off from their claims once they knew that their shenanigans would come to light.

Our God is a just God. He knows that he can administer justice better than we can. He also knows better than we do if our enemy is actually an enemy. He knows if their deeds ought to be punished or if it's really we who are out of line. He knows what amount of punishment is the correct amount. He knows what is best for the long haul and not just what is right for that particular moment. As the apostle

Paul said in 1 Corinthians 4:5: "Therefore judge nothing before the appointed time; wait till the Lord comes. He will bring to light what is hidden in darkness and will expose the motives of men's hearts. At that time each will receive his praise from God."

What Do We Do When They Come to Kill Us?

God knows that if we act in a manner becoming of the love of Christ, we can turn an enemy into a friend. Our enemy might never be exposed to Christ except for what he or she sees in how we act during a confrontation. If we let God do the correcting, we can be the force of love in the equation, balancing out the correction with encouragement. You could impact someone's life eternally with how you respond to whatever attack you perceive at the moment.

I recently attended a Bible study with a gentleman who works with Christian missions around the world. He told us of someone he was working with in an African country that is split 50-50 between Christians and Muslims. While the cities are peaceful, the outlying areas can get violent because of the two groups.

When our study group leader traveled to Africa to support this man and his friends, the Christian townspeople asked him a tough question: "If God calls us to love our enemies, what do we do when they come to kill us?" The Muslim side of town would raid the Christian side at night to steal their homes and kill anyone who would not submit. These people had seen members of their families killed over their Christian faith during these raids—only to have to literally walk past the murderers the next day on their way to work.

I don't know for sure how I'd respond to either the question or the situation if someone came to kill my family. But I do know that this man chose not to escalate the violence. He chose not to retaliate. As a result, there are key members of the Muslim community who have taken note and are now starting a dialogue with him about his Christian faith.

God doesn't call many of us to die for our faith. He doesn't call many of us to walk past our family's murderers and extend forgiveness. But I know that I am humbled beyond compare when I think of this man's faith and his Christlike nature. If he can do that, I can surely forgive someone's harsh comment in a meeting. I can learn to reduce the level of conflict in my business. I can learn to be gentler in matters in which my life is not on the line. I can turn my anger and my human nature over to a God who knows how to handle it all better than I could ever imagine.

For Reflection and Discussion

1. Is there anyone in your life whom you have not been able to forgive?
2. What kind of revenge fantasies have you concocted in your mind over the years?
3. When you became aggressive and vengeful at various times in your life, how did that work out for you?
4. How would you have responded to Lot if he wasn't willing to leave your land? How would you respond to another family member today if he or she wanted the home you had worked so hard to build?
5. Do you think that God really delivers justice if we give him the room to do so?
6. Is judging someone as right or wrong a vengeful act?
7. Is it true that forgiveness makes people healthier?
8. How can we know when it's right to stand and fight and when it's right to yield to an attack?
9. How would you answer this question: "What do we do when they come to kill us?"

Preparation for the Week Ahead

Rent the movie *War of the Roses*. Observe what happens when revenge becomes the primary motive in life. If you were in that situation, how might you have reduced the level of conflict? Would you have been willing to just walk away? What might you have done to keep the conflict from escalating in the first place?

In addition, observe what's going on in your mind this week. How much of your time is wrapped up in self-centered thoughts? See how much time you spend getting upset at other people for infringing on your time, space, money, business, and family.

How much do you think about getting back at people for what they've done to you? How much time do you spend complaining about who has done this or that to you?

What if you released all of it to God? Could he fix everything, including delivering justice on your behalf? Observe how you think and feel differently when you give it up to God.

A Prayer for the Week Ahead

Father, it is such a relief to know that I don't have to be the force of justice in every situation. It is good to know that even when you call on me to act, you are the primary force behind my actions. Help me to see that most people I think of as my enemies are truly not.

Cause me to see that my life can be a Christlike example to all the people around me, including my so-called enemies. Help me to see when I complain or gossip or plot against my friends, my family, or my coworkers that I am only hurting myself—and I am certainly not helping those upon whom I am heaping my rage.

You dwell with me, and yet I act as though you are not here. Cause me to remember that you are always with me. Would I gossip around you? Would I plot revenge around you? Would I say hateful things about others around you? I think not. And yet I do.

I am a sinner and have fallen so very short so very often. I ask that you help me to see this in myself so that I can begin to turn it around. Give me the strength to be compassionate, even to those who are not at all compassionate to me. Give me a heart of forgiveness, even for people who do not seek it from me. Give me a spirit of love, even for those who are unlovable. It is in Christ's name that I pray. Amen.

9

God Goggles

PRINCIPLE 9: *Love as Christ loved.*

Everyone who loves has been born of God and knows God.
Whoever does not love does not know God, because God is love.
— 1 JOHN 4:7-8

I did not want to write about love as one of the ten principles, but I knew I had no choice. Love is the most important of the ten, and it's also the one I struggle with the most in my daily walk. To write a chapter about love would only highlight the massive gap between what I know to be true and what I actually do. It's painful, and it's perhaps the thing I pray about more than anything else. So when it came to this chapter, I procrastinated for months.

That isn't to say that I don't feel love. I get weepy when it comes to how much I love my wife, children, parents, sister, friends, and extended family. Sometimes the love I feel for them overwhelms me. I would do anything for these people and would not feel a bit of sacrifice. I get more pleasure out of making them happy than I do when I'm focused on meeting my own needs. With them, I experience every day how powerful true, unconditional love really feels.

But when I apply that same standard to many other people I encounter, I fall way short. While I feel compassion for people in need,

I can't seem to love them in the same way I love my family. While I have come to be less judgmental of others, I still don't feel love for people I would consider evil, lost, hateful, bitter, lazy, or ruthless. And while I no longer feel disrespect for people who don't meet my high standards, I still don't feel love for them.

So here's my dilemma: Christ tells me that my behavior is no better than that of the average nonbeliever: "If you love those who love you, what reward will you get? Are not even the tax collectors doing that? And if you greet only your brothers, what are you doing more than others? Do not even pagans do that?" (Matthew 5:46-47).

Not only did Jesus encourage love for people outside our direct circle, but he also lived it in his every action. He died for me—an egotistical sinner. He allowed himself to be tortured, mocked, and killed by people just like me so that I might have everlasting life. He saw in me what I don't see in myself and thought, *He is worth saving. I will die for this man. I love him even though he is driving nails into my hands and feet.*

I still cannot fathom how our Lord could feel that for me, mostly because I don't yet understand how to feel it for people other than my friends and family. I would die for my family, but I could not picture myself dying for the guy who sits next to me on the bus. I'll go to the ends of the earth for my wife and children, but sometimes I won't even pick up the phone for the average person. I very much love the people I work with but not the people I drive past on the way to work.

I don't get it. I don't feel it. I've never "been there, done that." I don't have the T-shirt, and I didn't want to write about it. I'm thick-skinned. I have to be. I run a multibillion-dollar business, and I can't get too upset about the bad stuff or too gushy about the good stuff. I'd go insane if I felt every emotion about the things that come across my desk. As a result, I just don't have any business telling other people how to love others in the workplace because I don't always feel it myself.

But if I focus too much on *feeling the emotion* of love for people I don't particularly care for, I might miss the point. If I keep waiting to feel it before I demonstrate it, I could be stuck in this place forever.

I'd never get started. We saw earlier how God shows up when we step up; maybe the same principle is true with love. Maybe God will help us feel love when we start acting in a loving manner.

I experienced this while having lunch with a friend. I agreed to the meeting out of friendship, not because of any particular sense of commitment to help. I enjoy this person's company, but I did not really have time to meet about this subject, and I had several other pressing matters at work. But halfway through the conversation, she said something that took our conversation in a very important direction.

She had been burning about something a friend had said about her faith. It gave us an opportunity to discuss how my friend's faith journey was really going at that moment and how she felt about her walk with God. As the conversation unfolded, I could sense the Holy Spirit moving amid our discussion. I felt an intense desire to be of service at that moment and could feel how God loves, even if just for a brief moment. I'm sure I got more out of the conversation than she did.

While that incident would be important in and of itself, it takes on even greater meaning in view of what I had been praying for during that same week. Around that time, I had lost my intensity on spiritual matters. I was praying, but I didn't feel anything when I prayed. I was reading the Bible, but I didn't feel the excitement of picking up the Word. I had lost my sense of spiritual passion, and I had been praying to get the passion back.

My prayers were answered when I stepped up instead of passively waiting for something to happen. I felt the feeling of love *but only after I had been loving*. I felt the Holy Spirit only after I moved to share his kindness with someone else. I didn't feel it before that lunch appointment, but I sure felt it afterward—and it sustained me for a long time thereafter. It made me realize that while emotions are part of our human experience, emotions should not and do not drive us 100 percent of the time. *We should serve whether we feel it or not*.

In my human limitations, I cannot possibly love the way God wants me to love—at least not on my own initiative. But when I allow God's Spirit to move within me, he will love others through me in ways that

I cannot possibly initiate or sustain on my own. In the process, he might allow me to feel it—he might melt my hardened heart. But at times he might also remove the emotional component to see if I will still obey him and love someone when I don't feel particularly loving.

As I was preparing to write about the subject of love, my wife sent me a note for our wedding anniversary that directed me to 1 John 4:7: "Everyone who loves has been born of God and knows God." In fact, 1 John is filled with guidance on love. The following verses helped get me in the right spirit to consider this subject:

> Anyone who claims to be in the light but hates his brother is still in the darkness. Whoever loves his brother lives in the light, and there is nothing in him to make him stumble. (2:9-10)

> Anyone who does not do what is right is not a child of God; nor is anyone who does not love his brother. (3:10)

> This [love] is the message you heard from the beginning: We should love one another. (3:11)

> Dear friends, let us love one another, for love comes from God. (4:7)

> No one has ever seen God; but if we love one another, God lives in us and his love is made complete in us. (4:12)

> God is love. (4:16)

> We love because he first loved us. If anyone says, "I love God," yet hates his brother, he is a liar. For anyone who does not love his brother, whom he has seen, cannot love God, whom he has not seen. And he has given us this command: Whoever loves God must also love his brother. (4:19-21)

> This is love for God: to obey his commands. (5:3)

While John spends more time on love than most authors in the Bible, perhaps the best-known biblical statement on love came from the apostle Paul in his first letter to the Corinthians. We've all heard 1 Corinthians 13 read at virtually every Christian wedding we've ever attended. I had read this passage many times over the years but never really paid attention to it. It had become like most things we hear repeatedly: We read the words, but we don't really internalize them. We get the message intellectually, but the essence of the message never travels the critical eighteen inches from the head to the heart. We hear the words spoken at weddings, but we start looking at our watches and wondering if it will all be over soon.

One day, I read 1 Corinthians 13 again in an entirely new light. Something broke through and gave me a new perspective. Instead of beer goggles (which stands for a drunken, worldly view), I had God goggles on this time. I suddenly saw it. *I had been praying to feel love, but God first wanted me to understand what love is.* Up until this point, love had been only an emotion, a feeling. God wanted me to go deeper than a feeling. He wanted me to see what real love looks like.

What Real Love Looks Like

First Corinthians 13 is God's definition of love. If I can't feel love for the average man or woman on the street, I can at least follow this roadmap while I grow into a more loving Christian. And even if I don't experience the emotion of love, God shows me how I can demonstrate love. As the saying goes, love is a verb. It's obedience to God's command to love others. It's based on action, not on feeling.

Please join me for a fresh look at Paul's love letter. I'm going to ask you to read it this time with a new lens, a new pair of eyes—perhaps even a new heart. Take time to meditate on it, pray about it, and think about it throughout the day, the week, the month. I'm excited that you might realize the same truth that I did.

> And now I will show you the most excellent way.
> If I speak in the tongues of men and of angels, but have not love, I am only a resounding gong or a clanging cymbal. If I have

the gift of prophecy and can fathom all mysteries and all knowl-edge, and if I have a faith that can move mountains, but have not love, I am nothing. If I give all I possess to the poor and surrender my body to the flames, but have not love, I gain nothing.

Love is patient, love is kind. It does not envy, it does not boast, it is not proud. It is not rude, it is not self-seeking, it is not easily angered, it keeps no record of wrongs. Love does not delight in evil but rejoices with the truth. It always protects, always trusts, always hopes, always perseveres.

Love never fails. But where there are prophecies, they will cease; where there are tongues, they will be stilled; where there is knowledge, it will pass away. For we know in part and we prophesy in part, but when perfection comes, the imperfect disappears. When I was a child, I talked like a child, I thought like a child, I reasoned like a child. When I became a man, I put childish ways behind me. Now we see but a poor reflection as in a mirror; then we shall see face to face. Now I know in part; then I shall know fully, even as I am fully known.

And now these three remain: faith, hope and love. But the greatest of these is love. (1 Corinthians 12:31–13:13)

Love in Real Life

My "aha!" moment with this passage came when I was talking with my daughter about a relationship issue. She was going through a breakup, and her former boyfriend was being horrible. He was being insulting, manipulative, destructive, and inappropriate. In the past, she would have acted just as horribly in return, but she was maturing and knew that such childish, tit-for-tat backlash was not good for anyone. She also needed to calm *me* down about some of the things the guy was doing.

I pulled out 1 Corinthians 13 and read it with her, knowing that God's definition of love was where we should both direct our attention. But as I was reading aloud, I also realized how much I, in more subtle ways, had been acting like the bad boyfriend with some people around me. My actions might not have been as overtly childish and mean, but they were just as selfish and rude. This conviction drew me even more deeply into the Scripture passage and caused me to spend a lot more time there during the next month.

We all tend to make excuses for our behavior and to justify our poor responses. "If you only knew what he did to me," we might say, "*then* you'd understand why I'm acting this way." But God doesn't cut us any slack in 1 Corinthians 13. He doesn't give us room to rationalize poor behavior and lack of love because of whatever our circumstances might be at the moment.

I could tell you more stories here, all of which resoundingly demonstrate that I'm no expert, only a fellow struggler, in this crucial area of life. But the main point I'd like to make is that it's not about our stories, our reasons why. *In fact, our stories are a big part of the problem* as we vainly attempt to blame everything we say, think, or do on circumstances: what happened to us, what she did to us, what he said, the economy, the whatever.

First Corinthians 13 doesn't say, "Love is patient, except when your boyfriend is being a jerk." It doesn't say, "Love is kind, except when someone cuts you off in traffic." It doesn't say, "Love is not easily angered, except when your spouse does something for the umpteenth time that really bothers you." It just doesn't give us any room to use our stories (no matter how dramatic or justifying they might be) as excuses for acting with anything short of unconditional, Christlike love. Look again at love's definition:

> Love is patient, love is kind. It does not envy, it does not boast, it is not proud. It is not rude, it is not self-seeking, it is not easily angered, it keeps no record of wrongs. Love does not delight in evil but rejoices with the truth. It always protects, always trusts, always hopes, always perseveres.
>
> Love never fails.

Is that definition contrary to my human nature? Absolutely. Convicting? You bet. But I was starting to see just how dramatically my world would change if I could begin to love like this—from my most intimate relationships with my family to casual daily encounters with people I might never see again to business exchanges with customers and vendors and even to interactions with people I might have formerly called my enemies.

If this Scripture passage isn't a guide to perfect love, I don't know what else is. Imagine treating your associates, customers, and vendors as Paul prescribed. What if the annoying person at work or your difficult customer or tough boss felt this kind of love from you? What if the government operated with these values or if unions and management came together with this definition of love in mind? How quickly would the posturing and name-calling cease? How quickly could we resolve issues?

At this point I can hear someone thinking, *Enough of this bleeding-heart liberal stuff. I thought we were talking about business. I don't get paid to love people—I get paid to produce results. Get off the soapbox and tell me why any of this matters to my business.* Fair enough. I have two thoughts for those who feel this way, one spiritual and the other secular.

Thought 1: If our goal is to bring God into our workplace, then we'd better know what God's priorities are. His Word makes it abundantly clear that love is one of his top priorities. It's what Christ commanded us to do in John 15:17 (and in many other places): "This is my command: Love each other." We have been given our primary directive. If we want God to show up and do miraculous things for us and through us, then we need to follow his clear direction even if it doesn't appear to be good for business—and especially when we do not feel like it.

Thought 2: I would argue that companies with a 1 Corinthians 13 value system do better over the long run than companies without it. We saw this earlier with Jim Collins' reference to the most effective, Level 5 type of leader. And I've seen it many times in my thirty-year career.

In one company where I worked, we saw a dramatic turnaround in performance when we built upon such a value system. The business was quite large. We had more than 1,000 customers and more than 35,000 associates/employees. Within a business that big, some of our units operated within a culture built on the biblical definition of love. We also had plenty of units that operated from a more traditional, worldly system.

Over time, we noticed that our customer retention rates were significantly higher among those units operating with loving values (combined, of course, with sound financial discipline) than among the units with a more controlling culture. Our employee turnover rates were also much lower in the units where leadership took a more loving approach. When we saw this dramatic difference in results, we set about institutionalizing a more caring value system across our entire business.

Of course, in a secular world we could not speak in spiritual terms or even in loving terms. We also could not teach people how to love. That's something very personal to each employee. But we could model good behavior and tell stories about how the successful leaders were running their businesses compared to less successful leaders. Our training focused on values such as respect, trust, dignity, diversity, education, development, encouragement, support, transparency, and open dialogue.

We also began to celebrate our frontline associates in a very public way. Each week we published heroic stories of how they were saving lives, both literally and figuratively. We had fewer than fifty stories submitted in the first year, but within five years we had literally thousands of stories about our people doing amazing things for their customers and fellow associates. All stories chronicled loving acts of kindness in which our employees took the initiative to rally around someone in need. They helped inspire even greater acts of kindness throughout the entire business, a spirit that continues to this day.

We built these values and expectations into our management policies. We structured salaries and bonuses based upon how our associates felt about the leadership of their supervisors. New associates would often write to me to say that after working at several different companies, they now felt like they were home, that they had found their true purpose and vocation. Within five years, associate loyalty was up 60 percent, and turnover (losing associates to the competition) was down 25 percent. Our profits grew by 87 percent, and our customer satisfaction improved by nearly 40 percent. We did all this while saving our customers hundreds of millions of dollars in the process. Many years later, I still receive cards and emails from former employees who tell me that that particular company was the best work experience in their career.

But while I was very proud of that performance, I would soon be humbled during a conversation with a potential client worth hundreds of millions of dollars. When we went to meet with these people for the first time, we were greeted by four leaders who could not have treated us with greater respect. While we had important business to discuss, they were more interested in us. They wanted to know who we were and what our culture was about. They wanted to learn about our families and our backgrounds.

When we shifted the conversation to business, they began with a prayer to ask God to guide the meeting. They asked God to keep their team and ours mindful of how many people rely on us and how important it was that we take care of those entrusted to us. They asked that we be able to find common ground that would enhance the lives of the people we would serve together.

As we proceeded to talk business, the tone of the meeting had nothing to do with what we could do for them. It was more about what we could do together to better serve our combined associates and our mutual customers. They needed us to save them money, but that was secondary to the larger purpose of being good stewards for our companies, our people, and our customers.

During the visit, I presented our prospective five-year plan. We take long-term planning very seriously, and we're usually way ahead of our competition, so by the end of my presentation I was feeling pretty good. Our prospective client thanked me for my time — and then said something that humbled me to my core. Without even a hint of arrogance or superiority, he casually mentioned that when they think about long-term planning, it's in terms of hundreds of years, not five or ten years. They want to be good stewards for generations, not just until the next leadership change.

This group is one of the largest customers in their industry. They also happen to be one of the most successful. They are well-funded, they have cash (which makes them unique in their business), and they have plenty of power as the world would view it. But they view that power as God's power, simply a vehicle with which to express God's love.

Building a culture of love into your workplace can have a very successful, very secular impact on results. But that starts from a place where financial results are not the primary goal. When we come from a sense of loving service, it not only brings peace and harmony into the business, but it brings abundance as well.

For Reflection and Discussion

1. How do you define love?
2. My friend Dan paraphrases 1 Corinthians 13:2 this way: "If I have new accounts and profits and position and power, but have not love, I am only a _____." How would you fill in the blank?
3. Why do you think that love is the "primary directive"?
4. How did Jesus model love during his ministry?
5. How do you model love with your family?
6. How do you model love with your coworkers?
7. How do you model love with complete strangers?
8. When you interact with people, what does your behavior tell them about you?
9. Do you think that complete strangers feel your love for them?
10. Do you treat people the same when you're speaking on the phone as you do when you're speaking in person? How about when you're online or in the car? Do you think that God sees a difference between how you act when you're in person versus when you're on the phone or computer?

11. How do you model love when dealing with your child as compared to when dealing with people who report to you?
12. How do you model love when dealing with your boss?
13. Is it possible to be a strong leader and loving at the same time? What three traits would such a leader exhibit?

Preparation for the Week Ahead

Try to keep track of how you feel when you're in the presence of someone you love, and then compare that to your attitude when you're with a complete stranger. If there is a gap, why? How would you begin to close the gap?

Be of service to someone this week, even if you don't feel like it at the time. Notice how you feel. Do you get a brief glimpse into what it means to love your brother or sister as Paul defines it in 1 Corinthians 13?

Read 1 Corinthians 13 again, this time with a twist. As you read, wherever it says the word *love*, substitute the word *Jesus*. Then read it a second time, and wherever it says the word *love*, substitute your name. It'll sound something like this:

Jesus is patient, Jesus is kind. He does not envy. He does not boast . . . Jesus always protects, always trusts, always hopes, always perseveres. Jesus never fails.

Now read it with your own name inserted:

Scott is patient. Scott is kind. He does not envy. He does not boast . . . Scott always protects, always trusts, always hopes, always perseveres. Scott never fails.

If you are anything like me, you'll feel excited about replacing the word *love* with the word *Jesus*. You might even have an "Aha!" moment when you do.

But I bet you became uncomfortable putting your own name in the mix. As you read that version aloud, how far off the mark did you feel? I felt miles away, but it really showed me what I need to work on.

A Prayer for the Week Ahead*

Father, I know I will never understand how to give love to another until I understand what your love toward me looks and feels like. Please bring that kind of unconditional love my way so that I can see it face-to-face. Then please reveal to my senses and my mind what only my spirit can comprehend.

I read your Word and understand how wide, how deep, and how long your love is for me. I pray that from your glorious, unlimited resources you will give me your mighty inner strength through your Holy Spirit. And I pray that you will be more and more at home in my heart as I trust in you. May my roots go down deep into the soil of your marvelous love. And may I have the power to understand, as all God's people should, how wide, how long, and how deep your love really is. May I experience your love, although it is so great that I will never completely understand it. Then I will be filled with the fullness of life and power that come only from God.

Now glory be to God. By your mighty power at work within me, you are able to accomplish infinitely more than I could ever dare to ask for. May you be given glory in the Church and in Christ Jesus forever and through the ages. Amen.

*This prayer was inspired by Mark McGoldrick and used by permission.

10

Brian's Prayer Dare

PRINCIPLE 10: *Be persistent on your journey.*

I will not let you go until you bless me.

—GENESIS 32:26

And will not God bring about justice for his chosen ones, who cry out to him day and night? Will he keep putting them off? I tell you, he will see that they get justice, and quickly.

—LUKE 18:7-8

Although I've considered myself a Christian for as long as I can remember, my faith never meant much to me until I was in the eleventh grade. That was the first time Christianity came into my awareness as something worthy of my attention (I know how self-centered that sounds).

Up to that point, I had done little more than go to church every now and then. At best, I knew what it meant to go to church, but I knew nothing of Jesus or what he meant to me. I never even thought about it.

Then, while I was attending boarding school, there was a fellow student who lived in our dorm and who was the resident Jesus freak. His name was Brian, and he would often talk to us about what it means to be a Christian. Unfortunately, no one wanted to talk about Jesus, so Brian was pretty much shunned by our group.

One night, Brian came into our dorm room. My roommate and I did our best to escape, but Brian had us cornered. He went on and on about his faith. It's sad to admit, but I did my best to make him feel stupid for his beliefs. I'm not sure why I acted that way as I had no particular problem with Christianity, but I got in Brian's face about it. But no matter what I said, he continued talking about how faith in Christ would make a huge difference in our lives.

I told Brian to prove it. He looked me in the eye and said, "I'll tell you what. You pray for something and make it really unique and seemingly impossible, so that when it comes true you will know for sure that it was an answered prayer."

I accepted Brian's challenge just so he would change the subject. Finally we moved on to another conversation, not really giving the dare any further consideration. I don't remember how much time passed from the moment he challenged me until the time I actually did it, but I do remember being in class one spring day when the big prayer moment came.

It was nice outside, and the windows were open. Class was dull, and my mind was wandering. I was thinking about everything except what the teacher was saying. That's when Brian's prayer dare came to mind. I was bored beyond belief, so I thought I'd give it a try. But now—what to pray for? I must have thought about a hundred possibilities. I can still picture myself sitting in that chair, processing all the different things to ask for. Then I remembered my father's watch.

The Elusive Watch Pin

My dad had given me a watch that was too big for my wrist, but I wore it anyway because it was special to me. Because it dangled on my wrist, it would bounce back and forth on my arm. As it bounced, a wristband pin would occasionally fall out, but somehow the band itself would not come undone until it got knocked off, sometimes several days later.

Because the pin would fall out long before the band fell off, I'd lose about ten pins a year. I could be miles away from the pin before I even realized it had fallen to the ground.

Because I was away at school, I had to wait until I'd go home for vacation to get the watch fixed. I couldn't wear the watch without a band, so I walked around all day long asking people what time it was. (Believe it or not, we had no cell phones or computers then.) In this particular case, the band had fallen off a week earlier, and I wasn't scheduled to go home again for another two months, so I was looking at eight weeks with no watch.

So there was my prayer! "God, help me find the wristband pin." This was definitely impossible. The school had more than fifteen buildings on a very large campus, and during the course of a week I covered all that ground many times over. I'd been to hundreds of places since the pin fell out. The pin could be anywhere—lost in the acres and acres of grass, under my bed in the shaggy carpet, or swept up from a classroom floor by the cleaning crew. There was no way I was going to find it.

Finally the bell rang. I got up and half-wondered if anything would come of my prayer. My normal path from class was to take a left outside the classroom door, so I started in that direction. But then I realized that I'd left something in the classroom, so I did an about-face to head back. As I walked toward the door, something caught my eye on the floor in the distance, in the opposite direction from my normal route. I looked closely but saw nothing.

I retrieved what I needed from the classroom, reentered the hallway, and turned left again, glancing back at the floor where I thought I had seen something. Nothing. For some reason I continued gazing at that area, yet nothing was there. Then I noticed a small gap between the floor and the wall, covered in dust and cobwebs. I looked more closely into the gap but could not focus since there were a hundred kids in the hallway bumping into me while I was standing still.

Finally someone said, "Hey, MacLellan, move it!" I awakened from my daze and pivoted to walk back in the other direction. But then I turned around yet again and studied the crack between the floor and the wall. I crouched, peered into the crack, and reached with my index finger to clear away the dust and cobwebs. And there it was: my watch wristband pin.

I crouched there for a good while, brushing off the dust. I'm sure I looked a bit crazy down on the floor, rubbing a metal object like it was "My Precious" from *The Lord of the Rings*. My mind immediately began racing to explain what had just happened. *Of course I found it here*, I thought. *I come to class here all the time. It's only natural that it would have fallen off my wrist at this location.*

In retrospect, I can't help comparing myself to the man who was in a rush for an important meeting but couldn't find a parking space. He prayed to find an open space and was so rushed that he promised he would dedicate his life to Christ if a space opened up quickly. And just as he prayed that prayer, someone pulled out from a space right in front of the building, leaving him the perfect parking spot. Immediately the man prayed, "Never mind, I just found one."

That was me in that moment, explaining away the miracle as mere coincidence. "Never mind, Lord, I just found it myself." But still, it gave me serious pause. I walked to my next class thinking about the pin the entire way. By the time I sat down in my next class, I had prayed for all kinds of things, expecting immediate results. My impossible watch pin prayer was answered within minutes, so why not send up a thousand other prayers?

Of course, none of those other silly wishes was granted. I had been given my sign, and God was not going to let me turn him into a genie. That wasn't the lesson he wanted me to learn. The lesson was this: "I am here, so pay attention. Brian is right. Listen to him. Stop doing what you're doing and give your heart to me rather than the hundred other meaningless activities you engage in every day."

I wish I could say that I ran to Brian and told him how the prayer had worked, but I didn't. I didn't want to become his new Christian friend. He would never let go of me. He'd preach to me until we graduated, or so I thought. Instead, I kept the impossible answered prayer to myself and eventually let it fade into memory. I justified to myself that because none of the other prayers were answered after that big one, the watch pin prayer had been just a coincidence.

Still, that experience began a series of on-again, off-again miraculous occurrences that would cause me to really contemplate what a relationship with God through his Son Jesus might mean in my life. I have long referred to these moments as an angel with a two-by-four smacking me upside the head to get me to stop, listen, and obey. But mostly it's been a lifelong gentle nudging that has guided me in the right direction, day-in, day-out, pushing, guiding, and directing.

God has been persistent with me. He won't let me go, and for that I am eternally grateful. It was thirty-five years after my big watch pin moment that I really started to go deeper into my faith — thirty-five years of consistent, loving wake-up calls from God that got me to finally pay attention to what he was trying to tell me. It is only through his grace that I have been called into relationship with him, and I'm overwhelmed and humbled that he would pursue a man like me despite all the many times I have ignored or disobeyed him.

And just as God has been persistent in pursuing me, he wants me to be persistent in pursuing him. The Christian walk is not for the lazy or the faint of heart. It's the path of a pioneer. It calls for someone who won't turn back at the first sign of doubt or difficulty. It calls for someone who will stand up to his or her own demons and continue on God's path even though it can sometimes be a bit frightening.

Every Day Thereafter

Most of those who are new to Christianity think that there is only one big moment in their faith walk — accepting Christ as Savior. But in reality, there are two big spiritual moments every man or woman of God must ultimately face: (1) the day he or she accepts Christ and then (2) every day thereafter.

It's the second big moment, "every day thereafter," that many of us don't want to focus on because it requires a long-term, day-by-day, moment-by-moment commitment. God wants all of our time, not just a moment of it. He wants more than a single big decision. He wants our every thought, every word, every decision, every interaction, and every prayer. While accepting Christ as your Savior gets you into heaven, the rest of the journey is about bringing heaven to you while you are still here—and then to the rest of the world *through* you.

Jesus said in Luke 17:20-21, "The kingdom of God does not come with your careful observation, nor will people say, 'Here it is,' or 'There it is,' because the kingdom of God is within you." It is my opinion that persistence in pursuing Christ is what helps us find the kingdom of heaven within us and see how to let Christ live through us.

The first step, accepting Christ as our personal Savior, is *the* critical first step. But it's also an external, somewhat easier step to take. We hand everything over to Jesus and allow him to take the blame for our sin. It's Christ doing the work, and we simply sit back and toss our responsibility onto him. The second step is more internal. It calls for us to find something deeper inside of us, requiring us to die to our old self and become and live as the new creature that Jesus is making of us from the inside out.

That process of dying, or letting go, is difficult for most. The self dies hard—our flesh constantly beckons us back to our old life. We must be vigilant, constantly alert to the voice of God. We must learn to discern between what comes from the world and what comes from the Holy Spirit. For most of us, that will involve failing again and again as we learn how to hear the Spirit's voice and allow Christ to live and flow through us, even in the most difficult circumstances.

This might be the most frustrating part of the journey. I cannot tell you how many times a day I fail to act from a Christlike perspective and instead act from my own strength, my own mind, my own ego, and my own grit. I rarely purposefully disobey God any longer, but I frequently forget to even think about him and default right back to my worldly way of thinking. This allows the world to shape me rather than me allowing God's Spirit to shape me—and the world through me.

Watch Out for the God Facade

I wrote the opening pages of this chapter while on a plane, and the guy sitting next to me was not very friendly. He was rude when I got to my seat, and he was rude to everyone around him for most of the flight. My initial reaction was to let it pass. But after a couple of hours of his boorish behavior I began to think, *What a jerk. Who does this guy think he is?* I wanted to put him in his place and tell him what I was certain all of us were thinking by that point.

So there I was, writing a book about bringing God into my life, yet I was ready to let my old self take control and run *my* agenda with what *I* thought needed saying. I was writing to you about being persistent in the likeness of Christ, but my own persistence was fading as this man's rudeness wore me down. I was preaching to you about being persistent over your lifetime, but my own perseverance was showing a shelf life of about two hours. My politeness was only a God facade — my churchy self that might make it through the Sunday service but not through the ride home. The worldly me was ready to pop out and give my seatmate the what-for.

The good news is that I caught myself and realized that this man was really just one more lost person in our lost world. Who knows what he was going through that day? Whatever his situation, he seemed to be taking it on without any connection to a loving, powerful, personal God. Maybe I could be an example to this man — or at the very least I would not be an example of the world to him. So instead of appointing myself to put him in his place on behalf of everyone he'd offended, I opted to try to put his needs ahead of my own.

By the end of the flight, this same man was saying "please" and "thank you" to the flight attendant. We didn't become best buds, and he deplaned pretty much as surly as when he had arrived, but at least I knew that I hadn't made his situation worse. I also knew that my own persona while sitting next to him had transformed from one of judgment and rebuke to one of selfless service. (Situations like that can actually become a bit fun when you see them for what they are.)

If I hadn't been dwelling in the Word of God at that moment, I likely would have reacted from my flesh. It is only when I stay absorbed in the Word and in touch with Jesus through an ongoing spirit of prayer that I have the strength, faith, and wisdom to respond from a different place altogether. Just as being physically fit requires constant attention to eating right and exercise, staying spiritually fit requires one to stay connected to the Word at all times. That means staying centered on things that enhance your faith and walking away from things that detract from it.

This is the commitment that most people are not willing to make. It might mean that you'll have to stop watching your favorite TV show or that you'll need to change your music preferences or stop seeing certain friends who call you into a different lifestyle. You might need to stop reading only fiction or the newspaper and start reading the Bible. It might mean that you need to get up a bit earlier and start your morning with prayer and meditation rather than a cup of coffee and the morning paper.

These changes are all things that actually come quite easily once you are filled with (or controlled or empowered by) the Holy Spirit. I have now come to prefer these new activities over my old ones. But change did not come easily for me. It was initially much easier to do what I've always done at home, at work, and with friends. I had given my life to Jesus Christ, but nothing else had changed around me. It took years of God pursuing me and me pursuing God to create the beginnings of a change from my old way of living in the flesh to living from the Spirit flowing through me.

It required persistence for my behavior to catch up with the prayer I had prayed many years ago to receive Christ as my Savior and Lord. It requires persistence of me now. The apostle Paul wrote that he had to die daily, constantly leaving his old self behind and renewing himself in Christ. He confessed that he hated the old-self things he continued to do and that he knew that the Christian life was a never-ending battle to leave his sinful self behind. I think Paul and I could have had a lot to talk about.

Someone has aptly said that living the Christian life is not difficult—it is impossible. In human terms, that's so true. It's why God gave us the gift of his Holy Spirit. It is only as we yield our spirits to God's Spirit within us, moment by moment, asking him to guide, enable, and empower us, that the impossible becomes possible. True obedience is a gift from the Spirit. We cannot earn it. We cannot try harder. In fact, we need to try less. With the Holy Spirit on the throne of our lives, obedience simply flows through us.

I tried harder for years, and some of my greatest sins actually became more pronounced. It was only when I let go and relaxed into God that obedience followed. But it's a minute-by-minute thing. The moment I forget to let go and let God, my old self takes over, and I get surly and selfish and agitated.

Want Faith? Go Marry a Prostitute

One of the most interesting stories of persistence in the Bible is found in the first few chapters of Hosea in the Old Testament. Hosea, one of God's prophets, wanted to know how to love as God loves. And he learned pretty quickly that he should be careful about what he prays for.

As soon as Hosea prayed for love like God's, God told him to do something you would not expect. He told Hosea to go into town and find a prostitute—and then marry her. Hmmm. Now that's a conversation with God that belongs on *Jerry Springer*.

But Hosea did as he was told. He married the prostitute and, as you might expect, she was repeatedly unfaithful to him. She continued working as a prostitute. She had several children by other men and eventually ran off with another man. Hosea, heartbroken, lost track of her, but he later heard that she was being sold at auction as a slave. We're not told how she fell into this situation, but one could speculate that her other man, or men, had grown tired of her just as she had grown tired of Hosea.

So what do you think Hosea did? What do you think you would have done? I know I would have said, "That's it. No more of this self-imposed misery with that woman. She's nuts! She's unfaithful. She can't be trusted. She's a thief. She's arrogant and self-centered and unclean. And she's a prostitute. She deserves this lot in life, and I feel sorry for anyone who takes her on, even as a slave." I no sooner would have done anything for that woman than I would for someone who had mugged me on the street.

But when Hosea heard about his former wife's situation, his response was completely different: He went down to the auction and bought her back. No one else wanted her. Everyone else knew what kind of woman she was and wouldn't take her, even on the cheap. But Hosea did. He bought her back. Hosea was faithful because it's what God asked him to do, even though it required Hosea to humiliate himself. He did so even though it required him to give of himself to someone who had completely disrespected and abandoned him. Hosea was persistent with her.

God's parallel lesson for Hosea was that God persistently loves his people even though they prostitute themselves by abandoning him, living wastefully, and worshipping idols. God remains faithful even though his people do not. Eventually he would buy us all back at the price of his one and only beloved Son. And God remains faithful to us today, over and over again, even though we are often unfaithful to him.

Showing Up

At this point you might be thinking, *This is all well and good, Scott, but what about my work situation? Marrying a prostitute isn't going to look too good for me at the office.* Well, I'd have to agree with you that even this decadent world might wonder what's happened to your judgment if you show up one day with a prostitute on your arm. But I'm not going to ask you to do that. I'm asking you to consider how persistence can not only enrich your walk with God but also help you in your workplace.

Persistence is a secular principle as well as a biblical one. I'm sure you've heard story after story about the salesperson who overcame twenty objections to finally win the deal or the entrepreneur who failed at ten ventures before finally hitting it big. Persistence and sheer determination have led to many success stories over the years, and every one of those stories had to start somewhere.

Woody Allen once said that 90 percent of life is simply about showing up. Indeed, persistence starts with a single step: showing up. I cannot tell you how many people have shared their dreams and ambitions with me but have never followed through with even the first phone call, meeting, or business plan. They never go back to school, talk to investors, or look for the perfect location to start their business.

My twist on Woody Allen's statement is that 90 percent of people don't show up. They cower behind excuse after excuse until they convince themselves that their idea would have been impossible anyway. And among the 10 percent who do show up and take that first step, 90 percent of them drop out at the first sign of difficulty. Another 5 percent drop out once the second or third wave of trouble hits. That leaves only a very small percentage of people who show the strength and determination to succeed, whether it be in landing the job, the contract, or the new investor.

I was talking with a couple whose college-age daughter kept asking them for money. I suggested that they recommend to her that she search for a job to help pay for those extra things she wanted while at school. Several months later, the girl was still jobless, complaining about how bad the economy was and how the government needed to do something. When I asked how many interviews she had been on, they replied that she had searched Craig's List at least ten times during the previous few months.

That same young lady has since landed a position as a manager and is doing an awesome job, working very hard while attending school. But until she understood how "showing up" was necessary for people to see who she was and the attributes that she could bring, no job was going to hop from the Internet into her lap. Her perspective had been that other people were to blame for her lack of employment when, in actuality, all she had to do was show up.

Gee, This Would Be Fun

To give you a sense of what the average entrepreneur goes through to start a business, let me tell you a little story. My wife and I recently wanted to start a frozen yogurt franchise. So we started asking questions of the local operator and learned that he liked the business and would recommend starting one.

We began an Internet search and determined that there were five key players in the market. We went to each of those five companies several times until we narrowed our choice down to the two we liked the most. We visited various locations belonging to the two franchises many times over four months to determine who had the best product, who had the best marketing, and who seemed to be the most franchisee-friendly.

We visited both sets of corporate headquarters to meet with key management to see if we liked what they were doing with the concept. After all, it's the responsiveness and culture of the franchisor that makes or breaks a concept. One flight was three hours, and the other was five hours; each trip required about three days of travel.

We obtained the franchise disclosure document for each company. Each document was about 175 pages of legal jargon and financial data. We read through each disclosure document in detail to see what we liked and what we didn't like. We spoke with a friend who runs franchises to see what he thought about each contract. We hired a lawyer who reviewed them and offered his detailed legal advice.

By now, we were several months and several thousand dollars into the process. But wait — there's more. We conducted several conference calls with franchisees to learn about their financial models and returns on investment. We studied the industry trends to see if this was a good market for us to get into long-term.

We hired another lawyer to start up a limited liability corporation (LLC). We hired an accountant. We hired an architect and selected a builder. We opened a company bank account. Deborah spent three weeks scouting out the perfect location, which was five hours away from our house. But even that wasn't enough. We had to compete for the space because other businesses wanted the same spot. The developers wanted the most attractive business in their shopping mall. We were involved in several calls to prove ourselves to be their best option, which we eventually did.

Then we received the lease document, which was about fifty pages. We needed another lawyer to negotiate that agreement. Now we were finally ready to sign the lease, but the developers wanted a personal guarantee. The franchisor also wanted a personal guarantee, so we had to work with a banker to set up a line of credit, which required us to take out a mortgage on one of our properties. All this time we were searching for a manager whom we could trust to run the business with our $350,000 investment.

In the end, the entire deal fell apart over one paragraph (out of 175 pages) that we could not agree to with the franchisor. In our opinion, that single paragraph would have made the difference between financial success and financial failure for the business.

We still stop by the original frozen yogurt location to enjoy a treat every now and then. Often we overhear other customers talking about how great it would be to start a franchise. Deborah and I just smile. We know that most of these dreamers won't even remember their conversation the next day.

An entrepreneur would not only remember the idea, but he or she probably wouldn't sleep that night thinking about all the possibilities the business has to offer. They would study, plan, and execute. A lot of people talk about starting a business, but few people actually do. It takes persistence and hard work, and you have to kiss a lot of frogs before you find the prince of a business you always dreamed of.

The same is true if you're a teacher with a difficult student, a doctor with a patient you just can't seem to help, or a computer programmer trying to debug a program that no one has been able to fix. It requires a determination that stands up to challenges and a willingness to stick with it even if it's hard, grinding work.

Biblical Studies in Persistence

The Bible is filled with stories about healthy persistence. In many, Christ himself gives the examples of persistence and how it pays off with big dividends. Consider the following four scenarios:

In a certain town there was a judge who neither feared God nor cared about men. And there was a widow in that town who kept coming to him with the plea, "Grant me justice against my adversary." For some time he refused. But finally he said to himself, "Even though I don't fear God or care about men, yet because this widow keeps bothering me, I will see that she gets justice, so that she won't eventually wear me out with her coming!" (Luke 18:2-5)

Suppose one of you has a friend, and he goes to him at midnight and says, "Friend, lend me three loaves of bread, because a friend of mine on a journey has come to me, and I have nothing to set before him." Then the one inside answers, "Don't bother me. The door is already locked, and my children are with me in bed. I can't get up and give you anything." I tell you, though he will not get up and give him the bread because he is his friend, yet because of the man's boldness he will get up and give him as much as he needs. So I say to you: Ask and it will be given to you; seek and you will find; knock and the door will be opened to you. For everyone who asks receives; he who seeks finds; and to him who knocks, the door will be opened." (Luke 11:5-10)

Some men came carrying a paralytic on a mat and tried to take him into the house to lay him before Jesus. When they could not find a way to do this because of the crowd, they went up on the roof and lowered him on his mat through the tiles into the middle of the crowd, right in front of Jesus. When Jesus saw their faith, he said, "Friend, your sins are forgiven." (Luke 5:18-20)

Jesus entered Jericho and was passing through. A man was there by the name of Zacchaeus; he was a chief tax collector and was wealthy. He wanted to see who Jesus was, but being a short man he could not, because of the crowd. So he ran ahead and climbed a sycamore-fig tree to see him, since Jesus was coming that way. When Jesus reached the spot, he looked up and said to him, "Zacchaeus, come down immediately. I must stay at your house today." (Luke 19:1-5)

"I Won't Let You Go Until You Bless Me"

There are many more stories of persistence in both the Old Testament and the New Testament. Think about Moses and the nation of Israel wandering forty years in the desert to make an eleven-day journey, or think about Abraham, who waited twenty years for God to fulfill his promise that Abraham would become the father of many nations. Abraham was one hundred years old when that promise was fulfilled. Can you imagine how many times he must have doubted whether God was really with him?

Perhaps the best examples of persistence and the lack of persistence come from two brothers, Jacob and Esau. These two were the sons of Isaac and the grandsons of Abraham. Both had the potential to access God's incredible promise to build his earthly kingdom through Abraham's family line, but only one of the siblings would show the determination to claim it.

Esau was the eldest brother, and that mattered a great deal back then. The oldest son usually received the father's official blessing as well as the vast majority of the estate. Esau had access to that birthright and all the good that came along with it, yet he was impulsive and easily distracted. One day after hunting, Esau came home famished. His brother Jacob had made some stew, and Esau asked for some. Jacob agreed, but only if Esau would give Jacob his birthright—an outrageous request.

But Esau agreed! He gobbled up the stew, and two minutes later it was gone. Esau had traded the permanent for the temporary; he was willing to give up the promise of God for a momentary craving.

Rather than stay true to the long-term vision of what God wanted for his life, Esau succumbed to his short-term desire for something to eat.

The stew, of course, is symbolic of everything in this world that tempts us away from God's promise for our lives. It might be money, power, legal problems, an illicit sexual encounter, a flirtation at work, a lapse of integrity, a car, a house, a piece of jewelry, or whatever takes our attention away from the big-picture plan God has for us if only we'll keep our eyes on him.

Jacob had the determination to think long-term, and ultimately God's promise of a great nation would be passed down through him instead of through Esau. The promise culminated one evening many years later when Jacob was preparing to meet his brother after many years on the run. His hope was to reconcile with Esau, but he was very troubled over what might actually happen when they met. The Bible tells us that an angel came to Jacob and that they began to wrestle. Of course, the angel could have taken Jacob at any time. But he allowed Jacob to fight with him throughout the night.

At one point, Jacob got him into a lock and would not let him go. When morning came, the angel told him to let him go so that he might leave. Jacob replied, "I will not let you go until you bless me." With that, the angel renamed Jacob as Israel and revealed, "You have struggled with God and with men and have overcome" (Genesis 32:26,28).

And so the next time you are in the midst of a struggle, I want you to picture yourself wrestling with God. Let him know that you won't let go until he blesses you. He will reward your determination and your persistence.

"Why Won't You Let Me Fix This?"

I'll close the chapter with a personal story about our family's struggle with my daughter Amanda's illness. At the age of six, Amanda had already undergone one liver transplant, survived two cancers, and now was dealing with her third cancer. Our little girl was gravely ill. We took her home to die, and she almost did pass away one evening but made it through that night.

A few days later, Amanda became even more ill. I rushed her to the emergency room. She was septic, which means that bacteria were taking over her body and that she had no white blood cells to fight off the infection. Someone who is septic can die quickly, but he or she can also become violent and abusive. The aggressive behavior is a sign to the doctors that sepsis is present and potentially lethal.

We had been in the ER for two hours, and the doctors had been working on Amanda aggressively. This alone would have been hard enough, but Amanda was also fighting us the entire time. We had arrived at about 1 a.m.—it was now 3 a.m. I was exhausted, not only from this night but from the six years leading up to this moment. I had nothing left.

They were attempting to start another IV. We were on our fifth IV by that point, but because Amanda's veins were shot, none of the attempts were holding. This one failed as well. The staff went to start another one, and Amanda shot up to fight them off. As I struggled to hold her down, she went limp and fell back on the table. Again it appeared that this might be the end.

Suddenly the ER was filled with people. As each doctor or nurse came in to tend to my little girl, there was less and less room for me to hold on to her. Slowly, I was elbowed to the back of the room. I stood there for several minutes, watching the personnel do their work. And somewhere in that moment, I came to the end of myself. I ran into the ER bathroom, grabbed a towel, and screamed into that towel for about five minutes until I had nothing left within me.

Completely drained of strength, I fell back against the wall and sank to the floor. In one last outburst, I looked up at God and screamed, "Why won't you let me fix this?!"

I had never stopped believing in him, even amidst all the trauma. But that was actually my problem: I knew that God existed and that he cared, yet he had allowed all this to happen to my precious little girl. I could not comprehend the cruelty. I couldn't understand how a loving God could allow this kind of torture to continue.

But I was asking him the wrong question. It was not my place to fix the situation. The questions I should have been asking were, "How will you bless our lives because of this trauma?" "How can this be a blessing to you?" "How can I bring glory to you?" "What can I be doing to lead my family through this?" "What can I be doing to be a blessing to others with this?"

All those questions would ultimately be answered, but I could never give up seeking the purpose behind Amanda's suffering. If I had allowed my questions and bitterness to fester in my heart, I would be a different man today. I would not be close to God. I would not be experiencing his blessings. I would not know who he is.

But I had to keep coming back. And keep coming back. And keep coming back. Once I finally gave in and let God fix it, it was fixed. He patiently waited until I stopped trying to fix it, and then he fixed it. So my persistence had been misdirected. It was not my job to persist in being the one to fix the problem. My job was to persist in trusting God all the way through the trauma, even when all that I could see was the struggle.

Many years later, I met a young couple who had found out that the baby they were expecting would possibly be permanently disabled. This child had only 2 percent brain mass. Their prayer that day was not that God would heal the child (although those prayers would come later). Their prayer was not to end the pregnancy or to find some miracle cure. Their prayer was one of gratitude. The prayer they prayed that night was this: "Thank you, God, that you would trust us enough to love and care for a child with such special needs."

That is persistence in faith.

That is persistence that will be blessed for a lifetime.

It mattered not what the struggle was. It only mattered to this couple that God would be with them through it all. I'm pleased to say that their son is thriving and doing very well. He just celebrated his third birthday.

Hebrews 11:6 says, "Without faith it is impossible to please God, because anyone who comes to him must believe that he exists and that he rewards those who earnestly seek him." Those who are diligent, persistent, and faithful see the fruit of God's blessing in their lives, both at work and at home.

For Reflection and Discussion

1. What is the difference between changing from the inside out and changing from the outside in?
2. Can you change from the outside in? What would happen if you tried to change this way?
3. Can we earn our way to heaven through persistence? If not, then what is the value of persistence?
4. What is the difference between getting into heaven and bringing heaven into you?
5. Have you been persistent in pursuing God? How might you do better?
6. Think back on some recent hard times in your life. Have these traumas impacted your faith positively or negatively? Why?
7. How could some of your struggles be used to glorify God?
8. Have you asked God for a ministry of some kind? If so, have you taken the first step in that direction? Have you "shown up"? If you haven't asked for a ministry, why not? What are you waiting for?
9. What are your biggest dreams in life? Have you pursued them?
10. What excuses have you made for not accomplishing your goals?
11. What have you traded for your proverbial bowl of stew, as Esau did?
12. If you have accepted Christ as your Savior, how has your life changed since then? If your life has not changed, what are the barriers keeping you from taking that step?

Preparation for the Week Ahead

Keep track in the week ahead with how hard you have to try to be obedient to God's Word. Is it impossible to do it on your own? What happens when you let Christ live through you?

Also, look for how many times a day you make excuses for yourself, either for your behavior or for not succeeding.

A Prayer for the Week Ahead

Father, I am so afraid and so easily distracted from the road that leads to your grace. It is somewhat ironic that in order for life to be easier for me, I need to be persistent in pursuing you. I need to die to the flesh in order to live in the Spirit, which is a gift from you and something that really requires no effort at all. But it feels like work sometimes. It feels hard.

Help me to be persistent in yielding to your Holy Spirit's guidance and control and to accept the grace and love that come with it. With each breath, fill me with more of you. Consume me so that you are all I see, all I hear, and all I think. Help me to pray without ceasing, to be always mindful of your presence in my life and persistently aware of the gift you have given me. It is in Christ's name that I pray. Amen.

Epilogue

I started writing this book almost two years before I finished it, but it didn't take me that long to write it. The writing itself was probably only three months of nights and weekends strung together. The real reason for the delay was that God had a plan for me before I wrote this book. I just didn't realize it yet.

As I originally sat down to organize my thoughts about *Putting God to Work*, our company's results were so positive that we literally didn't know how to keep up with our cash flow. Our numbers were beyond everyone's expectations, and we were all feeling very good about how things were going. I wanted to write the book to give God the credit for all that had happened in our business and to talk about how easy life can be with God at the helm.

Wrong! The book I started to write and the book that got written were two completely different works.

Just a day after I started to make notes about the principles in preparation for writing, we received some bad news in the office. It was a painful account loss, but stuff happens in business, so it didn't seem particularly devastating or out of the ordinary. The following day, we learned some more unpleasant news, and the day after that came even more bad news. It no longer felt like the ordinary ups and downs of business. It was starting to feel like a significant storm was brewing on the horizon.

In the months that followed, I would get calls early in the morning and late at night, all with another wave of disappointing updates.

Sometimes the news was so dire and urgent that people were tracking me down in the bathroom. Before we knew it, $700 million of business was either lost or out to bid, and there were other matters even more serious.

How odd, I thought, that just as I was preparing to give God all the glory for what he had done in my business life, our results would suddenly come crashing down around us. I felt like a fraud. Clearly, nothing I had planned to write about was true. It seemed as if God was trying to show me that he cared nothing about the workplace and that he was making a huge point with this tsunami in our business. Clearly my basement breakthrough was no breakthrough at all.

As the tidal waves continued, I stopped writing for well over a year. I felt nothing at all about God's presence. In fact, I was miserable. Vacations were cancelled, normal family activities were put on hold, and I was either in meetings or on the phone about sixteen hours a day. Conference calls began at 6 a.m. and often ended well after 10 p.m. When we traveled on the West Coast, it was not at all uncommon to start our calls before 4 a.m.

Eventually our despair turned into a kind of gallows humor. We became so numb to bad news that we started chuckling with each update. We had felt all the negative feelings we could possibly feel, and now it was just funny that this disaster was so in our face all the time. But, truth be told, behind the nervous laughter my faith dwindled with each phone call or knock on my door.

After a year or so of this perfect storm, I pulled out the ten principles once again and read through them. They still spoke to me as true and right—even if the evidence around me indicated otherwise. In fact, the principles seemed to be even more tested and proven by the tough times we were going through. I started praying again to see what God was up to. I also remembered that my job is always to obey God regardless of whether I feel like it or whether I think he's helping me. My job is to trust the unseen despite what presents itself before me.

After getting back into my prayer and Bible reading routine, I began to see this difficult time as supernatural. I'm not sure if it was God presenting me with an opportunity to live by faith or if it was the devil having a Job-like smackdown with me, but something clearly was up. What had begun a year earlier had come on so quickly and was so severe and so devastating that I came to see that it wasn't possible for it to be just a coincidence.

It seems to me that this was the course I needed to run to make sure that I really believed in the principles I was about to share with you. It's easy to believe in godly things when everything is going well. It's much harder to believe in them when things are crashing around you and the world is at your door asking questions (and rightfully so) about your leadership.

I am happy to say that despite the massive negative trends, we still exceeded our plan during the months that these events unfolded. We had amazing (and I really mean amazing) things happen at the oddest times to help us survive. Eventually we saw waves of good news come in that seemed just as dramatic as the bad news had been.

It got me thinking about something that someone shared with me many years ago when I told him I wanted to enter the ministry.

"No, you don't," he said.

"But yes, I do," I replied.

"No, you don't," he said again. "Because the moment you enter ministry, you are entering spiritual warfare. Forces will come upon you that you cannot fathom or expect. Once you decide to pick up the cross, the journey will be difficult."

And he was right. As soon as I decided to take this message to the streets, so to speak, the trouble began. I might never know in this lifetime what good or bad forces brought the trouble, but I do know why. It was to make sure that I was willing to stand up to the challenge and stand firm in the beliefs that these principles do indeed mean something.

How to Start Your Workplace Ministry

I'm often asked this question: "How do you share your faith at work?" People will go on to say, "I work for a publicly held, secular company, and they would never permit me to talk about my faith or try to convert people on the job. I just can't see myself praying over somebody in the office and asking them to come to Christ."

I understand those concerns and concur that faith in the workplace is a bit of a balancing act for the average believer. But for the most part, you needn't do anything that would cause concern for a secular company, nor do you need to do anything that would put your HR department on high alert. In fact, I would suggest that *not* working by these ten principles is far more likely to get you called into HR. Principles such as these can serve as guardrails that keep you out of trouble while keeping you from making stupid mistakes at a company party or with a difficult customer.

You do not have to keep a Bible on your desk to live a life befitting Christ. Nor do you have to preach in cubicle doorways or baptize coworkers in the company fountain to show how much you love the Lord. My encouragement to you is to follow these ten principles without saying a word as to why you are living them — or even that you are working on them. Just *be* someone who lives these ten principles consistently, quietly, and confidently, and then see what happens.

At least for me, God's lesson has been more about living the Christlike life when the world is throwing everything possible at me. If I learn how to do that (and it's a lifelong process), I will quietly impact lives for the better even though the people who are affected might never know why. Along the way, I might even attract people to ask me what's different about my life, which then becomes my opportunity to speak openly about Christ.

Take a look at the principles in summary now. As you review them, tell me how many companies would have a problem with you if you did all these things quietly, confidently, in a nonjudgmental way, and without ever pointing out that you're doing them or why you're doing them.

1. Grow where you are planted.
2. Serve others more than self.
3. Humility is the first and most important ingredient.

4. Be tough. Be fair.

5. Access divine power.

6. Obey God. Abide in Christ.

7. Trust God.

8. Yield to attack.

9. Love as Christ loved.

10. Be persistent on your journey.

I know there are some aggressive, uncaring companies that might have an issue if you are "too kind" or "too patient" or "too loving." But I believe that most companies will honor and maybe even celebrate your actions if you live each of the ten principles at work. It is far more likely that people will gradually begin to recognize you as a positive example in their lives rather than as a Bible-thumping preacher to avoid at all costs.

I would also strongly suggest that your work ethic and your results will speak as loudly as your change in behavior. Remember that if you are not a reliable worker and are not successful at what you do, you will not attract people of the world to the Word of God. If you truly want to glorify God, he will use your diligence and success and life experience to his benefit. But if you just want to mark time for a paycheck, or even if you just want success for your own glory, then you have not gotten the message, and these principles won't work for you anyway.

Ten Steps to Getting Started

If you're not sure how to get started putting God to work, here are my thoughts about how you might take the first steps forward. Recognize that this is a journey and that you'll grow into this new approach to life over time.

1. **Start with yourself.** Before you try to share Christ with others, examine your own life and see if you are an example worth following. If you claim to be a Christian but act in ways

unbecoming of a Christian, consider who would want to follow you or the Christ you espouse. Don't try to take the splinter out of your friend's eye before you remove the beam from your own eye.

2. **Practice.** Get comfortable with the principles. They take practice. Work on them yourself before you try to teach them to someone else. This might take years. It's very easy to read about something that makes sense conceptually. It's altogether different when you actually have to apply it to a real-life situation, especially when you are under pressure.

3. **Don't preach.** No one wants to be preached to. Let your life be a living example of Christ's love. If your life attracts interest and people want you to share your faith, then do just that—share what it means to you. Don't preach about what it should mean to them.

4. **Don't be a chicken Christian.** It has become politically correct to avoid all reference whatsoever to God and Christian faith in the workplace. Don't fall into that thinking. Christianity is part of who I am, and I have every right to talk about my faith just as someone else has the right to talk about his lack of faith. Just don't be self-righteous about it.

5. **Let your life attract interest.** If you change enough, you are going to have people coming to you to ask why you have something different going on. I've been able to speak with hundreds of people about my faith because they've noticed its impact on my life.

6. **Let your results speak for themselves.** Once you deliver, the world starts to listen. God will use your success to attract attention. Once you perform, people will start asking how you got to where you are.

7. **Be prepared.** When someone finally asks you about your life and why you have faith, be prepared to answer that question.

8. **Invest deeply in a few people.** You are not looking for a bunch of seed sown in shallow ground. Rather than seeking

volumes of people who don't really get it, invest deeply in a handful of people. Ask God to use you to help change their lives at the soul level and then show them how to do the same for others. Then your ministry will multiply.

9. **Find godly counsel.** Everyone needs a mentor, a man or woman of God who can help keep you on track. Find that person or group of people who can support you along the way in your daily workplace ministry.

10. **Step up.** Take a step. Just go do something. Do what you can do and trust God to fill in the rest.

Look Around You

Your ministry is around you all the time. It's every person you meet, whether you know them or not. It's your spouse, it's your children, it's your team, it's your boss, it's your employees, and it's your employer. Don't look past the people in your immediate life while you wait to discover your ministry somewhere else.

If you feel called to a distant nation, you probably are called to go there; thank God for that. The world needs that. God wants that. But if you don't feel called in that way, maybe your ministry is right where you are. Maybe it's right at your desk. The people at work are just as real, just as in need, just as much a part of God's plan as the people you might travel thousands of miles to serve.

After you put down this book, make a list of all the places where you are a regular presence in someone's life. The list might include your home, office, club, fitness facility, battalion, church, neighborhood, extended family, suppliers, customers, or sports team. How could you be a blessing in each of these places? How could you show God's love?

Thank you for making this book part of your journey and part of your ministry. Please visit the website to share your story with us and to hear stories of your fellow travelers. We're in this together, so let's encourage one another. God bless you.

About the Author

Scott MacLellan is a successful entrepreneur and corporate executive. With thirty years in the working world, he has been either president or CEO of his company for thirteen years, including a technology business he founded, funded, and sold with two friends. Over the course of his career, he has held positions in operations, technology, procurement, marketing, and sales. Scott has received numerous awards for business excellence, corporate social responsibility, philanthropy, and associate engagement. His latest company was named one of the best places to work in healthcare and one of the top 125 training companies in the United States.

This is Scott's second book. His first, *Amanda's Gift*, chronicles the extensive illness of his youngest daughter. It serves as a how-to for other parents going through the illness of a child.

Scott sits on the boards of three nonprofit organizations and serves on the advisory council of several more. He mentors several young executives and often speaks to organizations about leadership both at work and at home.

Scott resides in Roswell, Georgia, with his wife, Deborah. They have two grown daughters.